NIGHT
BIRD

A Memoir

Shavaun Scott

Author's Note

This book deals with the sensitive subjects of suicide and inter-partner abuse. These are complex and multifaceted issues with deeply personal causes.

Many people who contemplate suicide are depressed, highly stressed, and hopeless. Some may be suffering from the delusions, hallucinations, or paranoia of psychosis. Others are in intolerable physical pain or terminally ill. And sometimes, suicide is on the continuum of domestic violence and motivated by rage, power, and control.

If you or someone you know is struggling with any of these concerns, help can be found by calling the National Suicide and Crisis Lifeline at 988 or the National Domestic Violence Hotline at 800-799-7233.

The owl, Scott's symbolic night bird, serves as both a harbinger of death and a bearer of wisdom, reflecting a deep emotional and spiritual journey.

FIRST EDITION, MARCH 2025
LIBRARY OF CONGRESS CONTROL NUMBER: *pending*
ISBN 978-1-965784-11-2 HARDBACK
ISBN 978-1-965784-12-9 PAPERBACK
ISBN 978-1-965784-13-6 AUDIOBOOK

Cover Graphic Design & Book Typography by Kurt Lovelace.
Cover artwork by Pierian Springs Press
Cover type *Bauhaus Dessau* **Alfarn** by Céline Hurka,
Elia Preuss, Flavia Zimbardi,
Hidetaka Yamasaki, and Luca Pellegrini.
Chapter titles in **Jenson** by Robert Slimbach.
Chapter titles in **Baskerville**; Body text set in **Nimbus**.
Chapter dropcaps set in **Mrs Eaves XL**
by Emigre Foundry designer Zuzana Licko.
Flourishes set in Emigre Foundry **Dalliance** by Frank Heine.
Emigre Foundry **ZeitGuys** by Bob Aufuldish, Eric Donelan.
Typefaces licensed Adobe, Linotype, Emigre, & URW GmbH.

PSPRESS.PUB
PIERIAN SPRINGS PRESS, INC
30 N GOULD ST, STE 25398
SHERIDAN, WYOMING 82801-6317

WITH GRATITUDE

Janet, Michael, Nancy, Bonnie, Syd,
Mashaw, James, Keshav, Adrian, Mike

CONTENTS

PROLOGUE

PART 1

1 | 911 3
2 | Aftermath 7
3 | Shock Treatment 11

PART 2

4 | The Edge of the Desert 21
5 | Sunday School 27
6 | A Cataclysmic Moment 31
7 | Annie & Jane 35
8 | The Cemetery 43
9 | Ornery Ida 47
10 | Mickey 51
11 | Sex Talk 55
12 | Tongues 59
13 | A Soldier for Christ 65
14 | The Dirty Boulevard 71

15 | Grandma Always Said 75

16 | Matrimony 79

17 | Blood 83

18 | Combustion 87

19 | The Missing 89

20 | Howling 95

21 | Rise Up and Walk 99

22 | The Willow Tree 103

PART 3

24 | Therapy 111

25 | Education 115

26 | Transitions 121

PART 4

27 | The Black Leather Jacket 125

28 | Togetherness 133

29 | For Victims and Survivors 137

30 | Nuclear Power 143

31 | The Search 149

32 | Faith and Hope 151

33 | A Resume 155

34 | The Color of Collars 159

35 | Valentine 163

36 | The Sacred Banyan Tree 165

37 | Truck Stop Diners 169

38 | The Cash Advance 175

39 | Talking Drums 179

40 | Mobile Crisis 183

41 | Reality Bites 193

42 | War Games 199

PART 5

43 | Robert—Back To The Beginning 205

PART 6

44 | Look What You Made Me Do 215

45 | Fine Transparent Vapors 217

46 | How May I Help You? 219

EPILOGUE

ABOUT THE AUTHOR 231

ALSO BY SHAVAUN SCOTT 232

NIGHT
BIRD

"One does not become enlightened by imagining figures of light, but by making the darkness conscious. The latter procedure, however, is disagreeable and therefore not popular."

C.G. Jung
PSYCHOLOGY AND ALCHEMY

PROLOGUE

My hometown smelled like exhaust and chorizo. The steel mill and freight trains belched black smoke into the sky. The dark gray air burned my eyes, leaving them permanently shot with crimson. If you tried to run, your chest hurt when you inhaled.

Breathing was dangerous.

People spoke Spanglish or hillbilly pidgin. Mariachis blew trumpets at weddings and quinceañeras. Everybody got drunk at funerals and, on weekends, swilled Bacardi from the bottle in the back of cruising low riders.

Girls who got raped after football games already knew how much money they would get from welfare if they decided to keep the baby. It was best not to cooperate with the DA since every criminal had at least one cousin who did hits; they'd get back at you if you snitched.

I was a permanent alien in my hometown. All I ever wanted was to run away.

But there were churches. Hallelujah, baptized, and born again. Churches with rock bands on Saturday nights, churches that were shimmering warm and bright, where the light was clean and holy, where God's family opened their arms to hug you, and they said they loved you, and everybody read the rules together from the same book.

You could be baptized in the Spirit and speak in tongues, get filled with the Holy Ghost, punctuate every sentence with "Praise the Lord," and trust that good things will come to those who wait.

In church, I learned there was no need to think about the future; just follow the blood on the tracks and trust God, who controls all things, even the temperature of the water that comes out of the tap. God, who numbers every hair on my head, God will take care of my life; no planning required, no thought required, just pray. Don't feel. Don't think. Just pray. Keep praying. Keep praying. Pray harder.

Pray until you're out of breath.

PART I

"But then, I suppose, when with the benefit of hindsight, one begins to search one's past for such turning points, one is apt to start seeing them everywhere."

Kazuo Ishiguro
THE REMAINS OF THE DAY

911

A Night in October
2004

My hands were shaking so badly that I had a hard time holding onto the phone, but I realized I had to hit three numbers to call for help. Time. Had. Stopped. Everything was suddenly wrong. It was dark, and the wind had picked up, sending the wind-chimes on the back deck spiraling. I was having a hard time thinking.

I paced in a circle with small, frantic steps as I hit three digits with my index finger. As I waited for the call to connect, I reminded myself to breathe. One ring. Two rings. Three rings. Then, finally, a male voice greeted me.

"Please send an ambulance," the words choked around the ragged sobs escaping from my throat. "I came home and found my husband—he's hanged himself."

There was a long pause on the other end of the phone, but I filled the void with sounds I'd never made before.

Finally, the man said. "Ma'am, this is 711. We're Repair. We can't help you. Maybe you should try 911."

"Oh, of course, I'm sorry," I said, ever polite. "I was trying to call 911. I'm upset. I'll try again." I hit the button to disconnect the call. "Breathe," I said aloud as the wind-chimes tinkled.

I stared at the shaking phone in my hand as the numbers swirled. My fingers were drunk. The shaking spread from my hands up to my arms and vibrated through the center of my body. I hit three more digits and waited much longer this time.

I could hear myself gasping for air, and the room was spinning. I was dizzy, weak in the knees—and cold as if I'd suddenly fallen into ice water. One ring. Two rings. Three rings. Four rings.

Finally, I heard a woman's voice. She sounded kind, and I was relieved. "Please send an ambulance. My husband is dead. I came home and found him hanging, and I don't know what to do."

"Ma'am, you've reached directory assistance at 411—you need 911."

"OH SHIT!" I sobbed.

"Ma'am, I'll put you through to 911. Just hold on."

While the wind shook the house and rattled the windows, I kept pacing, shaking, and trying to breathe.

Then, out in the driveway, on my knees with sharp gravel pricking the skin of my bare legs, I held the phone to my ear, and there was a new man on the line who kept saying, "Calm down, ma'am, calm down!"

The part of me hovering above recognized that he was being absurd. No one ever calms down because someone tells them to. I understand these things because I'm a therapist.

Aftermath

The Dirty Bomb
October 2004

"Michael, she's completely regressed," Janet whispered. I could hear her speaking on the phone in the hallway next to my bedroom, where I lay curled into a fetal position under a thick, down comforter. My friend Janet and her husband Michael, both psychologists by profession, were in their late 60s and retired. They lived 350 miles away in Palm Desert, but she'd driven all night to get to my home on the Central California Coast when she'd heard about the suicide the week before. Warm-hearted and good-humored, Janet was like an older sister to me. She hadn't left my side since she'd arrived.

"She won't eat, can't sleep, all she does is cry. She blames herself. God damn him! This is awful."

There was a pause.

"Oh, it was an elaborate production. You know how theatrical Robert was. He left a poster-sized sign on the front door, directing her where to find him—the house was dark except for a spotlight shining on his body."

Another pause.

"Yes, I've called all over. Santa Barbara, Ventura, L.A. I even tried the Menninger Institute in Kansas. No psych hospital will take her for PTSD unless she's suicidal. She's not. And even if she were, they would only keep her for three days. Insurance won't cover it. It wouldn't be enough time to do her any good."

It was terrifying to witness myself unraveling. I felt like an untethered astronaut floating backward into space, staring wide-eyed into the darkness, knowing that my oxygen was thin and even though people were around me, no one knew how to get me more air. I kept drifting further and further backward into the void.

Robert's smiling face kept appearing in my mind, along with the constant accusation: I killed him.

I sobbed and shook and retched. I spoke perseverative nonsense until my throat closed. The small hard ball that became my stomach refused to accept food. The stranger in the mirror frightened me, and I tried not to look at her.

My eldest son and his wife came 170 miles to deal with the coroner and take care of the burial arrangements. My 21-year-old son took the train home from college in Berkeley and slept next to me in my bed while I fought my nightmares. He cut up pizza into small bites with a fork and tried to feed me one bite at a time. My daughter came and drove me to therapy, where I met with a befuddled woman who had no idea how to help. Friends brought food that I couldn't eat and didn't want. I told everyone it was my fault he was dead.

It was impossible to get warm. Shivering constantly, I dressed in layers despite the temperature in the 80s. I wore thermal underwear covered with a flannel shirt and a suede coat over that, baggy flannel pants, and thick socks inside of bulky Ugg boots. This was my standard outfit every day and night for weeks. I cocooned under an electric blanket, yet still, I shivered.

Even with double-dosed Ambien, sleep was never more than an hour at a time. I would wake from nightmares of trying to breathe life into Robert's dead body while I screamed at him, "Why?"

Lighting white candles, I talked to ghosts at night. Convinced my house was haunted, I left messages for a psychic who never returned my calls. When barred owls called mournfully from the pine tree outside my bedroom window, I was convinced they carried messages from the dead that I couldn't understand.

I didn't want to die. But I didn't know how to live.

"Michael," Janet said, "She can't care for herself. I want to bring her home to us."

Shock Treatment

November 2004

Janet was hoping for a touch of levity, and she sang along with Dolly Parton songs as she drove us south down the 101 freeway in her old white Volvo on the road to Palm Desert. She thought the singing might cheer me up, but I'd never cared much for Dolly's music and couldn't bring myself to smile.

With my eyes closed, I reclined in the passenger seat and focused on the monotonous thrumming of the tires on the roadway. I sunk low into the seat, wishing I could disappear.

"Okay," Janet said, "let's try something else. I want you to imagine being surrounded by a warm white light inside a big titanium bubble. You're safe in there, and it's quiet. Let all the noise in your head fade away."

Recognizing her switch to a therapeutic metaphor, I went along with it. I preferred the stories to listening to her sing along with Dolly's *"The Best Little Whorehouse in Texas."*

If you hang out with a psychologist when you're in crisis, you'll get any number of creative interventions. Janet and I had met ten years earlier when she'd briefly lived on the Central Coast and joined my small therapy practice. We shared a cozy office with a fireplace, a blue velvet couch, and a view of the pine trees. Janet wore her empathy like a gentle cloak, ready to embrace anyone needing warmth, and she made everyone feel seen and valued. She and her husband, Michael, were known for taking in stray humans in need. Michael, who primarily did forensic evaluations for the court system, was the pragmatist, and Janet was Mother Earth. They made a great team.

I'd lost 15 pounds in a month and had no appetite or energy. My arms and legs felt leaden, and things like brushing my teeth or combing my hair took more energy than I could muster. My guts twisted up, and my chest hurt with every breath.

The warmth of the sun cutting through the car window felt good. "Look at the ocean out there; it's so beautiful," Janet said, but my eyelids were leaden weights, and I couldn't keep them open.

It was a six-hour drive, with traffic slowing to a crawl through the Los Angeles basin. A familiar stretch of California, I had no urge to see it again. I could have driven it like an old song I knew too well.

About an hour and a half southeast of LA, we neared my hometown. I shifted my body completely away from the window. It was a place I intentionally remembered to forget, and we still had two more hours of driving to go. I pretended to sleep.

It was a relief to finally arrive in Palm Desert. Janet

had a small room lined with bookshelves near the back of her beautiful home, with a narrow twin bed covered with a red quilt and an electric blanket. "Here," she said, "we've made you your own room, and you'll have occupational therapy with me. You can lie in bed under the electric blanket if you need to, but I want you to listen to audible books as much as you can. I have a whole selection of Tony Hillerman stories. And every day, you have to get up and do something – you can help me re-pot plants or walk down the block to get the mail. You can walk around the backyard pool whenever you want. The thing is, you have to get up and do something at least once every day. And I'll be here to talk whenever you need me."

She knew I couldn't go far since I was unsteady when walking.

Outspoken and fatherly, Michael had known Robert for years; he knew we'd had conflicts. He tried to break my trance of guilt and took every opportunity to encourage me to be angry.

"Damn him!" he'd say vehemently, "This was about contempt, a neon sign created for you – you had reasons for wanting a divorce, and he was mad about it. People get divorced all the time. Robert had a better life than 90% of the world, and how dare he throw his life away because he was angry!" I couldn't respond. None of it seemed real.

"I'm just glad he didn't kill you too," he said, "you know I've seen those cases in my forensic work. Sometimes, an angry guy will shoot his wife, then himself. Sometimes, they even kill the kids."

Michael said I was lucky to be alive but didn't feel

lucky. At that moment, I would have preferred that Robert had killed both of us.

I lay curled up in the little bed with headphones on, listening to hours and hours of Tony Hillerman and the adventures of Jim Chee. I refused food, and Janet came in every few hours to check on me. After two days, I wasn't getting better, and she was worried.

"I went online and found a psychiatrist from the Central Coast who will consult with you over the phone," she said, sitting at the foot of my bed. "I know you've got the antidepressant and Ambien, but they're not working. If you work with this doctor, you can follow up with him when you get back home."

I agreed, and we scheduled a phone call for later that afternoon.

"Dr. Walker, she's not usually like this," Janet said when she spoke to him, perched on the end of my bed. "She's a high-functioning woman. But since it happened, she's been agitated and has not been sleeping. She's got obsessive, circular, perseverative thoughts—she's overwhelmed with guilt. Well, here, you talk to her, and you'll understand."

I spoke hesitantly to the doctor for fifteen minutes. He was warm and compassionate, but I was muddled and had trouble answering his questions. He asked to speak with Janet again.

She took notes on a small spiral pad as they spoke, then turned to me when they hung up.

"Dr. Walker says you have severe PTSD and delusional grief with psychotic features. Do you understand me? You're not seeing reality right now. All this self-blame isn't called for. None of us believe you killed Robert.

Robert made his own decisions, just like he always did. You are not responsible."

I had a hard time accepting what she said. I knew I was supposed to believe her, but I couldn't find a way to push my thoughts out of the rut they were stuck in.

"Look at all the weight you've lost—my God, you haven't eaten any solid food in weeks. If we don't get this turned around, you'll need to go in the hospital due to malnutrition."

"I'll do whatever he suggests," I said. I longed to feel better, but I was mired in misery and couldn't find my way out.

"He wants you to stop the antidepressant for now because you must get some sleep—depression can be treated later, but sleep is the priority. Sleep will help your brain recover. He's calling in a prescription for a major tranquilizer along with the Ambien. We'll pick it up right now."

When I looked at the bottle of pills later that evening, I recognized the name of a familiar antipsychotic medication. I'd had clients on it, but it was not a category of drug I'd ever taken. But I was game.

After I swallowed one of the oblong white pills with a half-glass of water, I felt something shift within the hour. It was like the relief you feel when loud, jarring music hurting your ears is muted. The tormenting thoughts grew softer. My thinking became clearer and less confused, and breathing felt less painful. And I felt hungry for the first time since the night Robert had died.

"I think I can eat something," I said to Janet as I walked out in the living room. Michael threw together spaghetti for dinner, the best thing I could ever remember eating.

☙ ☙ ☙

I can say that shock therapy eventually saved my life, but in my case, the shock came three weeks later from accidentally falling into the deep end of Janet's swimming pool while wearing my thermals, flannels, suede jacket, and Ugg boots. Those thick suede boots instantaneously filled with water, and I sank right to the bottom. The cold water shocked me and knocked the air out of my lungs.

From the bottom of the pool, I looked up through the water above me and saw the blue sky. Far away, I could hear Janet screaming, "Michael, help! She's fallen in—she's drowning!"

I became aware at that moment that I had a choice to live or die—and instantaneously, I was conscious of choosing to live. I would fight for breath; there was never a doubt. I pushed up off the concrete bottom with all my strength, flailing through the water in my wet coat, and as my face finally broke the surface of the water, I realized I was laughing.

I was laughing so hard I almost swallowed water. I laughed because Janet was hysterical, and I was worried about her blood pressure. I laughed as Michael ran out of the house with blankets and towels. I laughed as I shed the outer layers of clothing beside the pool. I was laughing that I had almost drowned because I was not in my right mind; I was overdressed, and the medication I took had left me just unsteady enough not to realize I was stepping backward right into the swimming pool when Janet had decided that I needed some fresh air. I had laughed because poor Janet was trying so hard to save me, and now she felt responsible for almost drowning me.

Something about the shock of that cold water spurred my desire to live, and suddenly, the muscles of my heart, mind, and limbs started to work together with my brain. I was alive. My laughter proved it.

And for the first night in weeks, I slept more peacefully. I was on my way back.

PART II

"Nothing of me is original. I am the combined effort of everyone I've ever known."

Chuck Palahniuk
INVISIBLE MONSTERS

The Edge of the Desert

1960s

The hot Santa Ana winds blew an army of tumbleweeds through the neighborhood. The air at the edge of the Mojave Desert was crackling and dry. As a child, I chased the tumbleweeds down wide, lonely streets into the nearby sandhills, imagining that one day, the wind would carry me away to a soft, green, forested place with clear blue skies.

My hometown community was known as the Inland Empire, but no trace of magnificence could be found there.

My lean, red-haired father was a truck driver and proud to be a Teamster. He drove 16-wheelers seven days a week. My petite, red-haired mother had gotten her GED in her twenties and then graduated vocational school as a phlebotomist. She liked drawing blood.

Though my mother had given birth to three other children two decades earlier, she gave birth to me at age

36 after her first children were grown and gone. She returned to work when I was ten days old, and I always yearned to see more of her.

She left me with her parents, who lived next door in a one-bedroom cinder block cottage with a tin roof that leaked when it rained.

Grandpa and Grandma's house had rectangular windows amid rectangular blocks, like an old Mexican jail. A swamp cooler in the largest window filled the space with a loud, steady hum every summer. In the hundred-degree heat, I ran through the yard sprinklers to get damp, then came in to stand directly in the blast of the cooler.

The large console black and white television dominated Grandpa and Grandma's front room; it came on precisely at 8:00 am and didn't go off until 10:00 pm when they went to bed. They each had recliners facing the TV; next to Grandpa's chair was an empty Folger's coffee can known as his "spittoon."

I sat cross-legged in front of the TV on the bare floor while we watched reruns of Gunsmoke, Beverly Hillbillies, Divorce Court, and my favorite—Roller Derby. I jogged in a circle around the living room, pretending I was a Kansas City Bomber.

I wandered back and forth between the cottage and my parents' adjacent house, a beige stucco three-bedroom with a roof covered with white rock that was supposed to help keep it cool in the summer. A few blocks away, the freeway traffic droned, and the freight train wheels clacked parallel to our street, carrying hobos up and down the Golden State.

"C'mon now, youngin', time to feed the chickens and

collect the eggs," Grandpa would say every morning at 9:00 am. I'd follow him back to the chicken coops beneath the walnut trees on our half-acre, carefully settling the eggs in an old wicker basket as he slipped them out from under the hens.

Grandpa wasn't much for conversation, and he chewed tobacco as we did the morning chores.

"Get the hose over yonder," he'd say as he spat. "I reckon it's time you learn to help." Watering the rows of tomatoes and corn, I pulled a green rubber hose through each section until the soil grew muddy and dark, clinging to my bare feet and lower legs in layers.

Like generations before him, Grandpa had been a farmer in Kansas and Oklahoma in his younger years, with Grandma and their kids working by his side. Born in 1892, Grandma had grown up on the Caddo Indian Reservation. "We didn't have electricity until 1940," she'd told me, explaining kerosine lamps, outhouses, and life before airplanes and indoor plumbing.

At least a couple of days a month were fried chicken day, and Grandma would catch a fat white hen and wring its neck as the poor headless thing ran around the yard, spurting blood.

"You can cover your eyes, girl!" she'd yell as I climbed up the walnut tree in the middle of the yard to distract myself.

When the noon meal was served, there would be chicken fried up in Crisco, crunchy battered okra, and sometimes, my favorite, fried cornmeal mush.

I'd wander outside alone if it wasn't too hot in the afternoons. Blue violets and red geraniums grew around the perimeter of Grandma's house, and I imagined tiny, beautiful fairies in gauzy chiffon dresses living among the flowers, like the ones I'd seen in Disney movies.

Crows circled overhead, and I spoke my thoughts aloud, talking to myself.

My first memory is when I was hospitalized at fifteen months old because the pediatrician thought I had leukemia. The leukemia turned out to be nothing more than anemia because I'd always had straight cows' milk in my bottle, with no added iron or baby formula.

"We didn't know what to do with you," my mother told me years later, shaking her head.

"You wouldn't eat food; you only wanted your bottle."

In an old photo album, there's a studio portrait where I'm three years old, wearing a black and white checkered dress. My bright orange hair was curled at the shoulders, and trim, short bangs ran straight across my forehead. I'm smiling at the camera, and my small teeth shine silver. I'd had bottle mouth syndrome as a toddler because it was Grandma's habit to leave me in the crib for hours with a bottle of milk propped in my mouth, which rotted my baby teeth. All my teeth had to be capped with silver when I was three.

I was a solitary child. When I started school, it was hell. Small, pale, and skinny, my orange hair and sunspot-covered face made me a target. "Freckle-faced Strawberry" was a regular taunt, which caused me to blush bright red, only bringing more taunts and laughter. I repeated the word "Ugly" whenever I saw my reflection, a habit that went on for decades.

At night, I'd cry that I didn't want to go to school in the morning because the kids were mean.

"There, there," my dad would say, his drawl elongating

each word as he patted the top of my head. "It don't matter none. Don't listen to 'em."

I knew better than to complain to my mother. Whining to my mother always resulted in a bad outcome. She was an unpredictable, hard rubber ball of anger, and as she put it, "I do not abide whiney kids."

Sunday School

1963

I was proud as I recited to my mother. "For God so loved the world that he gave his only begotten son that whosoever believeth in him shall not perish but have eternal life. That's John 3:16," I said.

She beamed. It was rare to see her that pleased. As a five-year-old, I showed quite an aptitude for memorizing scripture. I desperately wanted her to be proud of me.

My mother firmly believed that all children needed to attend Sunday school to develop moral character, even though she didn't participate herself. Above all, children had to be well-behaved. Mom saw the morality and obedience of her children as a direct reflection of her character, and the church could scare them straight better than anything.

There happened to be a Southern Baptist church two blocks away, and beginning at age four and a half, she dropped me off every Sunday promptly at 9:30 am for the 9:45 children's class. Mom always thought it was important to be early for things; lateness was one of many sins.

I always wore one of my better dresses and fancy white patent leather shoes reserved for church. When she returned to pick me up, she'd inevitably scold me for scuffing the shoes.

Miss Julie was a plump and pleasant teacher. Since it was a tiny church, there were never more than three or four of us in the classroom, sitting in little plastic chairs under bright fluorescent lights facing a chalkboard.

Miss Julie smiled most of the time, except once every Sunday when she talked about hell and the lake of fire.

"Everyone who doesn't accept Jesus into their hearts will burn in the Lake of Fire forever," She'd say, turning grim. We looked at each other as we imagined flames licking our bodies, crinkling our skin until it turned black, burning our hair away. That image stuck with me; I'd chew on my fingernails when I thought about it.

Every week, Miss Julie read a Bible story aloud. Jesus turns water into wine at the wedding. Satan tempted Jesus in the desert. Lazarus rose from the dead and walked out of the tomb. Jesus restored the sight to blind people and healed lepers with a touch. And, of course, the betrayal by evil Judas, the subsequent trial by the Romans, and the torture of the crucifixion.

Sin was a constant theme. Our sinfulness was what caused Jesus to be nailed to the cross with a sword thrust through his side. The thought of nails being driven through my hands and feet haunted me as I lay in bed at night. Falling asleep took hours and hours because I couldn't stop imagining the bloody holes in my body. I felt guilty that my personal sinfulness had caused Jesus to be tortured.

I vowed to work hard not to be sinful, but it seemed impossible because even having an angry thought was a sin that God kept track of. And God was always watching; he knew every thought we had and counted every single hair on our heads.

The idea that God was watching made me uneasy about bathing and changing my clothes. I covered up with a towel after taking a bath as fast as I could. Shame became my constant companion.

Miss Julie told us to be kind and joyous, to keep praising God, and to pray without ceasing. Above all, we had to tell others how to be saved by asking Jesus into their hearts so that they could be born again. We sang, "This little light of mine, I'm gonna let it shine." I took it seriously. We were all missionaries, and it was my responsibility to help save others.

"Jesus," I prayed, "you can count on me."

Everything was on my shoulders, but I was up to the task. I could make a difference. I could help save people from the Lake of Fire. I promised that I would never, ever let God down.

A Cataclysmic Moment

1965

"W-A-R-S-H" was the easiest word on the spelling test.

I was hard-headed, even in 3rd grade, and on that afternoon in September, I was incensed that my teacher was so wrong. Mrs. Craig had put a red check mark next to the word "warsh" on my spelling test. She'd made an error, and I knew better – I knew phonics, after all.

When I think I'm right, which is most of the time, I'm known to take a stand and hold my ground. Since I'd started talking at 15 months old, Grandma had accused me of arguing for entertainment's sake, and on that one thing, Grandma was right. But I'd never agree with Grandma out loud.

"If I said it was salt, you'd swear it was pepper," she'd say as I sat next to her on the plaid bench seat of her 1955 Plymouth. Grandma was only 4'11" and had to sit on a cushion to see over the steering wheel, which was so big it could have turned the Lusitania.

I was already an expert at eye rolls and peevish facial

expressions. My mother's pet name for me was Miss Smarty-Mouth, and she didn't say it affectionately. Though my grandmother tolerated my rudeness, my mother regularly slapped my face. On bad days, Mom used the wooden spoon or yardstick across my bare thighs.

There was a lot to argue with Grandma about, like how she called lunch "dinner" and dinner "Supper" or how she thought the stories about baby aliens in The National Enquirer were true. How she called the fridge the "ice box." Like my parents, Grandma hadn't gone to school past 8th grade; even then, it showed.

"We are poor people, honey; we've always been poor," was her default explanation when I asked her to explain one or a thousand things she said or did that made no sense.

But on that day in 3rd grade, after the spelling quiz, I was righteous and confident and not going to settle for injustice. I should have gotten 100% on that quiz because I knew how to spell warsh.

I raised my hand and took a stand. "Excuse me," I told Mrs. Craig in front of the class. "I spelled that word right, but you marked it wrong."

Mrs. Craig handled it well. She asked the other kids what they thought, and those who spoke up argued against me. "It's W-A-S-H," said Shelly, my best friend whose parents had gone to college and lived down the street. I thought Shelly pronounced some words funny, but I'd never said anything about it.

Mrs. Craig suggested we get the dictionary to look it up for ourselves, which didn't rattle me. I was confident I would be vindicated.

The cataclysmic moment came in less than five minutes when Shelly showed me the word on the page of the big classroom dictionary: W-A-S-H. "It's pronounced waaash," Shelly said.

"See, right here." I stared at the page and couldn't believe what I saw.

My face grew hot and red. I was shaken to my core. Somebody in the back of the room laughed and said, "Look! She's turning red." Several others snickered. Something was terribly wrong, but I wasn't sure what it was. It was a feeling that would stick with me for decades like a lingering, vague, unpleasant odor.

I was different from other people but couldn't quite understand why. Kids, even my friends, still giggled about my red hair and freckles. I stayed quiet in school and tried to blend into the background. I also made it a point to pay close attention to how my teachers and people on TV pronounced words, and over time, began to affect a slightly proper British accent. I studied my spelling words with religious dedication and never got another word wrong on a spelling test.

Annie & Jane

1960s and 70s

Annie was my mother's older sister, and she read fortunes for a living. When I was seven, Grandpa fell over dead in the garden from a massive heart attack. After the funeral, Annie took over the spot in his old recliner and sat with Grandma every day, watching Divorce Court, Dragnet, and Roller Derby.

Annie could divine meaning from regular old playing cards spread across a kitchen tabletop to determine whether or not a husband was prone to infidelity. She read tea leaves to predict if a firstborn child would be a boy or girl. Annie would advise you to improve your luck by putting a bay leaf in your pillowcase when you sleep or attract a lover by drinking tea made from ginger. When a mourning dove cooed three times in a row, Annie would say it was sure somebody close to you would die.

Annie saw patterns everywhere, and she knew how things were connected.

She had short, curly, copper-colored hair and ever-present gold hoop earrings that she never took off. When I was growing up in the 60s and 70s, she wore bold floral-patterned dresses she called shifts that hugged her ample curves and made me think of Hawaii. Her lipstick was always ravishing red.

Annie drove a blue Mustang, which she wrecked and replaced at least twice during my elementary school years.

She taught me to dance the hula barefoot on the grass in the backyard and convinced me there really was a man who lived in the moon with his wife.

"I'm a counselor, honey; I've always had a gift," Annie explained when I asked her how she earned money. "See that actress on Days of Our Lives—I read cards for her and her friends in Hollywood. I have a whole list of clients I help; they've come back to me for years."

Annie gave love-life advice to soap opera stars from patterns she could discern in formations of cards she'd been trained to interpret by an old Roma man she'd met at the Eagles Lodge where she'd been cocktail waitressing.

She made twenty bucks in cash every time she gave a reading.

※ ※ ※

Jane was my pious aunt, married to my father's hard-drinking brother. He had a reputation as a misanthropic alcoholic, but Jane was known as a woman of God. She was tall, blonde, rail thin, and straight-backed, with a small, tight smile that never revealed her teeth. Her lipstick was such a pale pink that you could barely see it. She wore crisp white blouses that she pressed with her iron. Jane inspired my admiration.

Jane drove a long beige station wagon with plenty of room for kids and groceries in the back. She never broke the speed limit. She was a stay-at-home mom who believed that the man was the head of the household and the breadwinner. She took care of everything else.

Jane had two daughters, one named Sarah, my age, and the younger, Hannah, who was always sick and whiney as a stray cat. Hannah was diagnosed with ulcers from "nervous problems" when she was seven, and always got attention by saying some part of her body hurt. Often, we saw her trip and fall on purpose and then wail for her mom as if it had been an accident. She was four years younger, and Sarah always tried to ditch her because she tattled so much. "Get lost, crybaby," Sarah would say.

Since Sarah and I were close friends as kids, I spent much time at their place while growing up. Sarah loved dogs, bikes, and climbing trees, the same as me.

As I got older, I went to church with Jane and the girls on Sunday mornings and often to the youth group on Wednesday evenings. God and the rituals surrounding him were the center of the home—which naturally excluded my uncle since he was unsaved and, therefore, destined for hell. According to Jane, so were my parents and all the rest of our relatives. Even those who professed to be Christians—like my mother—weren't living a Christ-centered life, which meant they weren't legitimately saved. My mother wasn't a churchgoer and didn't

try to lead others to the Lord, one of the most important signs of a real Christian. Either you were a real
Christian and lived every moment as an ambassador for
Christ, or you belonged to Satan; there were no gray
areas when it came to heaven or hell.

It was unsettling to find out my mother and father
belonged to Satan. I wasn't sure what to do about that
other than pray.

My Uncle Dan worked long hours as a truck driver,
just like my father, but he drank so much beer every
night that he went to sleep on the couch when he got
home. He didn't have any use for most people, especially
kids, and we knew to stay out of his way or risk a whip-
ping.

"Children are to be seen, not heard," Uncle Dan
stated at the dinner table, forming his words around a
cigarette in the corner of his mouth without removing it
to talk. He never smiled, and his eyes were dark and
mean.

Most of our family members were going to hell. I
prayed for them all at least six times a day. And I'd pray
in the middle of the night when I woke up with bad
dreams about Armageddon, the anti-Christ, and the
mark of the beast. Insomnia was always a problem.
There was so much praying to do, and I was never sure I
was getting it right. I put my whole heart into praying; I
could feel my chest tighten as I lay in bed at night, trying
to make sure God heard me. The devil was everywhere; I
could feel him in the dark, like a moth landing on my
hair.

Annie made me think of a bright monarch butterfly with ADD. She didn't spend much time in one spot. Her laugh was a little too loud, and her voice could set your teeth on edge. My dad complained about her over-talking and always letting the screen door slam.

In addition to the card reading and tea leaves, Annie could discern meaning from examining the lines in the palms of your hands. This fascinated me as a kid, and I was forever trying to have her show me the meaning of things that she could somehow see, but I could not. No matter how hard I tried, I couldn't see what Annie did.

She got me a Ouija board for my ninth birthday, but honestly, I had to admit my fingers moved the cursor where I wanted it to go. When I played it with Annie, it always told me nice things, like I'd marry a tall, handsome man with money someday. I believed her.

Annie owned every book the psychic Edgar Cayce had ever written and fancied herself a faith healer and a medium, but Grandma warned her to stop talking about dead people when company came.

She loved Las Vegas and had several lucky numbers that seemed to show up in significant patterns in ways only she understood. At one point, she began altering the spelling of her name to improve her luck. Anna, Annis, Annie, Anna Mae, Ann-with-an-e. Adding one or two letters could change the course of everything.

Jane's worldview came strictly from the Bible. All the sins were clearly and conveniently identified, and they included most normal human behaviors, including having things like emotions. Jane was talented at not feeling emotions herself. I never saw her cry or raise her voice; she never once spoke a curse word. Jane was even-tempered and didn't smile too big or laugh out loud. Even though my uncle was drunk and passed out most of the time when he wasn't at work, she kept to her steadfast routine and never seemed to be bothered by him.

Her home was oddly comforting; it was predictable. I always knew what we would have for lunch—bologna sandwiches, Fritos, and coke—and that we'd pray before we put a bite of food in our mouths. The house would be immaculate, and the laundry would be done. Jane kept to her schedule; she held the kids to their chores. Things were lined up straight. Just don't make trouble and do what she said. I respected her.

Whenever there was a problem, Jane would offer one reliable solution: prayer. She told us that life would work out fine if we served God. God had a special plan for each of us. She stayed busy doing God's work, saving her from worrying or even noticing so many things that were wrong.

Both Annie and Jane had magical thinking, though they did it differently. I looked up to them as role models and integrated their methods of getting through life. The message that stuck was that if you wish hard enough or perform the proper rituals, you are in control of what happens in life; if you can trust that there is a divine plan, you don't have to worry.

It all made life so simple. You just follow the formulas in the mystical books, and you'll get what you want. Good outcomes were guaranteed, and I clung to that. I needed to believe, just like they did.

The Cemetery

1960s

If you followed the tumbleweeds through the sand hills and beneath the railroad overpass scrawled with gang graffiti that read "Royal Lords," you'd arrive at the town's greenest haven—the cemetery.

Established in the 1800s, the cemetery was a striking contrast to its dry surroundings. Lush and meticulously maintained, its rolling acre of thick grass was shaded by tall cedars, sturdy pines, and the delicate limbs of pepper trees. No matter how hot or dusty the valley grew, the cemetery always felt cooler, an oasis of shade. The spicy scent of the pines and pepper trees cut through the suffocating gray smog that often hung over the valley like a shroud.

For me, the green space always had a calming effect. The air felt denser there, in a comforting way, as if it held a secret weight that settled my mind. Though it was a place meant to contain the dead, it felt vividly alive.

Grandma and Annie spent a lot of time at the cemetery, and as a little girl, I often joined them. Family members who had passed on, many of whom lay beneath the very ground we walked on, still held a powerful presence in their lives.

Grandma's weekly ritual involved us gathering red geraniums or pink roses from her yard, arranging the stems in small jelly jars filled with water, and packing them carefully into a cardboard box. We'd ride in her Plymouth, slowly making our way up the hill to the cemetery. Once there, we'd walk in the dappled light, placing the flowers on headstones of loved ones who had been long gone before I was born. Grandma would tell me their stories as we went.

"My brother Jim died suddenly of pneumonia when he was 45, and his wife Ruthie followed him the next year. Aunt Molly lived to 93 but went blind before she passed. She had the diabetes too. She used to make the best homemade peach ice cream."

Grandma knew exactly where every gravestone lay and how each person was connected to our family.

If Annie came along, she would often shed a few quiet tears, dabbing at her eyes with a tissue while sharing her own memories. "I know they're still watching over us," she'd say. "I can hear their voices."

I believed her. In my imagination, the spirits of Grandma's relatives were grateful for our visits, and I spoke to these strangers in my mind, making sure they knew they weren't forgotten.

I was especially captivated by the older tall granite monuments, some adorned with black-and-white photographs of the dead. I'd study their faces, wondering what they were like in life and imagining their ghostly forms promenading through the trees in their finest after-dark attire.

By the time I was in second grade, I began visiting the cemetery alone after school, carrying a half-read book under my arm. It was less than a ten-minute walk from home. I'd wander the paths between the headstones, reading inscriptions and imagining the lives of the people buried there, pondering what had brought them to their end.

The cemetery was always quiet and rarely visited by others, and that was why I loved it. The solitude and silence were a balm for me. Eventually, I'd settle in a shady spot, leaning against a headstone with a Sherlock Holmes or Agatha Christie novel in hand, half-listening for the whispering ghosts I believed were watching me. Mysteries fascinated me, and reading felt as essential as breathing.

The peace I found in cemeteries stayed with me throughout my life. It's why *El Dia de los Muertos*, The Day of the Dead, remains my favorite holiday. The connection between the living and the dead, the honoring of those who came before—has always seemed comforting to me.

Ornery Ida

1967

I woke up at 3:00 a.m. with a pressing need to pee. Though I was nine, the dark still unnerved me. Stumbling toward the bathroom, I flipped on the overhead hallway light; my path illuminated just enough to navigate. But as I passed the shadowy living room, I froze.

Behind the green sectional sofa, a tall, dark shape moved, accompanied by low, incomprehensible muttering. My nine-year-old mind leaped to the worst conclusion—a murderous burglar. I stood there, paralyzed. Did he have a gun? Were we all about to die?

"HELP!" I shrieked, which sent my parents rushing from their bedroom at the far end of the hall,

But there was no intruder. Instead, crouched behind the couch was Aunt Ida, muttering to herself in the dark.

Ida had a habit of wandering the house in the middle of the night, hiding in strange places when her fears took over. She believed mysterious intruders were after her, when the rest of us were sound asleep. As my father quietly guided me to the bathroom and back to bed, my mother dealt with her younger sister, as she often did. The family had a simple way of explaining it: Ida wasn't right in the head.

"Ida, it's Mickey. There's nothing to be afraid of. Come on, let's get you back to bed," my mother said, her voice steady and authoritative. It seemed to work. She took Ida by the elbow, steering her back to the guest room at the far end of the house.

In Grandma's photo album, there was a black-and-white portrait of Ida from when she was twenty. She looked radiant—blonde, with shoulder-length curls, a dazzling smile, and a movie star aura. It was hard to reconcile that stunning beauty with the Ida I knew at 40.

Now, Ida frightened me, though I couldn't fully explain why. She was gaunt and stooped, her pale skin stretched tight over her frame. Her eyes, wet and unfocused, never met mine directly. Conversations with her were disjointed, and if I asked her a question, the response was usually a jumble of nonsense. The light behind her eyes had long since dimmed.

She also had a habit of rummaging through our things when we weren't home, often taking odd items that made no sense. I once found one of my Bobby Sherman albums in her suitcase, though she didn't even own a record player.

Ida came from Kansas to stay with us for weeks at a time, but no one ever explained why. Mom, Grandma, and Aunt Annie would talk about Ida in hushed tones. Grandma had raised some of Ida's daughters years ago, though the reasons for that were among the many family secrets no one discussed openly.

Ida's restlessness drove her to wander the streets of downtown during the day. One Saturday night, she returned with a man named Marv, disheveled and eccentric, whom she'd met near the bus station. Marv was rotund, with long, greasy hair and a fondness for wearing conspicuous turquoise jewelry. He lingered at Grandma's house for about a week before she came to my father one evening after dinner.

"Stanley," she said, "I caught Marv slipping one of my silver teaspoons into his pocket. I just fed him a meal of liver and onions, and he's not even grateful—he's a thief. I know what he's up to. He turns those spoons into rings and sells them downtown."

That was the final straw. My father's face reddened as he told Grandma, "I'll take care of it, Mary Pearl. You've put up with Ida long enough—her boyfriend needs to go."

The next day, Ida and Marv were gone. The sense of relief in the family was palpable.

Years later, my mother told me that Ida had been diagnosed with schizophrenia and was eventually placed in a state mental hospital back in Kansas. Shaking her head, she said, "We always thought Ida was just ornery, but it turns out she was crazy the whole time."

There was more shame attached to "crazy" than to "ornery." No one wanted to admit to the "crazy" genes, though we had them anyway. Growing up with Ida in the family made me endlessly curious about the human mind—what made some people so strange?

Decades later, I learned that Ida had given birth to 13

children in rural Kansas, but only five—all daughters—survived. The boys, including two sets of twins, died at birth. No one is sure where the bodies were buried, but it's rumored they were laid to rest somewhere in the yard, a secret held by the earth.

Mickey

1960s

Although my mother's given name was Delpha, she much preferred to be called Mickey. I never quite knew where the nickname came from, but I always suspected it was something assigned to her in school—perhaps a nod to her pale, freckled Irish complexion. Standing at just 5'2", she was slender, with delicate features that masked the fierceness of her temperament. By her thirties, she had begun keeping her thick, auburn curls cut close, opting for practicality over vanity.

"Stern" was Mickey's default setting. Even in family photos, her smiles felt stiff and rehearsed, as if she were forcing herself to fit an expectation she didn't care for. No matter how hard I try, I can't recall a single memory of her laughing. It always felt like she was holding on to life by her fingernails—those same fingernails that always seemed on the verge of breaking.

Mickey had a way of speeding through life, quite literally. She drove fast, avoiding eye contact with the neighbors as she zipped by in her blue Ford. If Mr. Crane, the old man across the street, happened to be outside, she'd avert her gaze entirely. "That old drunk will talk your ear off," she'd say, dismissing him. "As for Vera, the woman down on the corner, she'll want something," Mickey would grumble. She had no time for pleasantries or small talk. Her world was tightly sealed, and there was no room for casual friendships.

Friendship, to Mickey, was a nuisance. Any effort to cozy up to her only irritated her further. She didn't see the point. In her mind, Annie, her older sister, consumed all the energy she had to spare. Annie spent every day at Grandma's house right next door, drawing on Mickey's dwindling reserves of patience. Whatever was left over went to running the household.

On Saturday afternoons, Annie would read my mother's fortune at the kitchen table. I'd try to eavesdrop, but they whispered in hushed tones, keeping their secrets just out of reach. Afterward, they'd head off to K-Mart, returning with plastic bags full of little indulgences—a new top, some underwear, or plastic flowers that Mom would stick in the dirt around the house. "From the street, no one can tell they're fake," she'd say. "They brighten things up."

While new shopping malls with fancy stores had popped up across town, we never set foot in places like Nordstrom or Macy's. If we needed something nice, there was always Sears, and that was our limit. But Mickey loved K-Mart. The moment she walked through the doors, it was like a switch flipping, and she was energized.

Thrift stores, though, were off-limits. "That's where poor people go," she'd say dismissively when I asked about places like Goodwill or Value Village. To Mickey, making it to K-Mart was a symbol of success—a sign that she had worked her way up in the world.

Mickey became a grandmother for the first time at just 36, the same year she had me. By the time she was in her mid-40s, she had ten grandchildren, yet she never really got to know them in more than a superficial way. Each Christmas, she'd gift them the same thing—a sensible pair of flannel pajamas, always wrapped with meticulous care. Though she never cradled them in her arms or asked about their interests, she poured all her energy into wrapping each package perfectly, creasing the paper with precision, curling the ribbons just so. Gift wrapping had become something of an obsession for her, a skill honed after an old humiliation.

Years earlier, when she had first moved to California, Mickey had brought a gift to a coworker's baby shower. One of the women had laughed at her poorly wrapped present. From that day on, Mickey vowed never to be laughed at again. She practiced until she mastered the art, and any compliment she received about her beautiful wrapping was met with a retelling of that story, her voice tinged with quiet defiance. She refused to let anyone make her feel small again.

Mickey's toughness extended to me as well. When I was seven, a group of older boys at the bus stop started pelting me with dirt clods. I ran home in tears, expecting sympathy, but instead, I was met with her anger. "You fight them back!" she snapped, hands on her hips.

"I learned to fight boys when I was your age, and you'll learn to fight them too. Go back out there and hit them harder than they hit you." Her words hit me harder than the dirt clods had. I was smaller than all of them and had no defenses against a group of boys.

After that, I started faking stomachaches and headaches to avoid going to school. I learned quickly that telling my mother about anything bad that happened would only lead to me being blamed. Somehow, it would always be my fault. I had to toughen up, fend for myself, and learn that in my mother's world, there was no space for vulnerability.

Sex Talk

1960s–70s

"Watch out for Uncle Bill," my mother said when she'd cornered me in the laundry room on a Saturday morning. "He'll pinch your breasts." Her face was tight, and she looked angry. The smell of laundry detergent made my eyes itch.

I was puzzled. At ten years old, I couldn't understand why an old man would pinch someone on the chest, which is what I equated with "breast." My great-uncle Bill was Grandma's older brother, desiccated with yellow teeth, a shiny bald head, and a perpetual growth of gray stubble across his lower face. When he came to Grandma's house, he tickled me in concentric circles on my belly with a rigid index finger until it hurt, and I wailed for him to stop.

What did "watch out" for Uncle Bill even mean? What was I supposed to do—watch closely while he pinched?

I stood there, mute and embarrassed.

I do not doubt that my mother had prayed I'd be born a boy. It was dangerous to be a girl. And most importantly, boys didn't get pregnant. She stressed to me on multiple occasions as I got older that the birth control pill had been the most important thing ever invented in the history of science.

A year later, Mom cornered me again in the same spot in the laundry room, her jaw tight.

"Listen to me. Boys will try to touch you, and you can't let them. If you do, they'll pop your cherry, and when you get married, your husband will know. He won't want to be married to you anymore."

I felt like I was in trouble and flushed bright red. Baffled at what she was talking about, I decided she was crazy. After all, I thought many boys were pretty interesting. What was she so worried about?

My puberty timed with my mother's menopause, one year after the Summer of Love struck in California. Both of us were moody and volatile, driven desperate by opposing hormones. We agreed on nothing, and I rebelled against every command. She grew louder and more volatile while I became determined to defy her.

We didn't venture toward the subject of sex again until I got my first boyfriend the following year, in 7th grade. "You can't have a boyfriend until you're 16," she commanded after catching me in the kitchen talking on the telephone with him.

Desperate for any form of positive attention, I tuned her out. While my mother was at work, my boyfriend Alfredo walked me home from school every day. She had no idea what I did after school; by then, I had started avoiding Grandma's house and headed straight home instead.

Alfredo and I shared innocent moments—holding hands and stealing kisses. He wrote me sweet, childish love letters, which I guarded fiercely in a shoebox tucked under my bed.

In my daydreams, we would escape to Scotland and live together in an ancient, abandoned castle. I practiced writing my first name, followed by his last, envisioning a life filled with adventure and freedom.

Tongues

1972

By the time I turned 13, I regularly attended three different churches each week: a charismatic church on Saturday nights, buzzing with young people and Christian rock bands; the youth group at my childhood Baptist church on Wednesday evenings; and Sunday mornings at the Pentecostal Assembly of God with Pastor Raeburn. The more God you could fit into your life, the better.

Pastor Raeburn was the most captivating of the lot. Despite having spent his entire life in Southern California, he spoke with a thick Texas accent that made his words sound even more colorful. Short in stature, he sported a voluminous shock of white hair slicked back like Elvis. His gray eyes, as big as silver dollars, sparkled with electric energy when he preached, and his booming baritone had a lyrical quality, making his sermons feel like a vigorous form of poetry. Clad in a crisp white shirt beneath his black suit and tie, he always exuded the nostalgic scent of Old Spice.

He was the first person I ever saw speak in tongues.

"Ralaadaa—deemeeum—aadaakaa!" he would shout into the microphone, raising a fist toward heaven. The sounds flowed from him like music, a melodic combination of consonants and vowels. Through him, I learned that speaking in tongues was a sure sign of being filled with the Holy Ghost, a way to channel divine words directly from God.

Every twenty seconds, he would pause to translate the prophecies he claimed to receive. "Be holy, my people, and obey my word," he declared, as though he were the direct conduit to the Almighty.

Pastor Raeburn warned us of the demons that lurked outside the church, ready to lead Christians astray. "Satan is running the public schools, the secular universities, and those demonic scientists mislead our young people with their talk of evolution and fornication," he would preach. "Remain pure before the Lord and stay away from these things, lest you end up in the fires of hell."

Movies and music that didn't explicitly honor God were also of the devil. Even Disney films, he cautioned, were riddled with witchcraft and magic, making them unsuitable for viewing—something that confused me since I had always enjoyed them and my mother encouraged them.

The only safe course was to memorize Bible verses and stay focused on the way, the truth, and the life— meaning Jesus. Over time, the voice of the Lord in my head began to sound just like Pastor Raeburn.

Faith healing was a significant part of the Assembly of God.

"If you are saved and have faith, you will not get sick," he insisted. "It's the devil that causes sickness. If any of you are ill, it's a sure sign of a faith problem—or a direct demonic attack."

I couldn't help but ponder: if no one ever got sick, then why would anyone need to die? If that logic held, it would mean Christians could live on Earth forever. Why, then, did we even need heaven?

Yet, I knew that such thoughts were dangerous. Questioning my spiritual elders could lead to the unraveling of everything I believed, a terrifying notion.

My mind became a labyrinth of incantations and prayers as I fought to avoid independent thinking. "Trust in the Lord with all thine heart, lean not unto thine own understanding; in all thy ways acknowledge him, and he shall direct thy paths." *Hallelujah, Jesus.* I had to remain vigilant and focus solely on the word of God. *Praise the Lord.*

I diligently took notes in the margins of my Bible at every church meeting, capturing the pastors' interpretations of each verse. My Bible became heavy with multicolored ink, yet I struggled not to notice that the pastors from different churches often disagreed on what God was saying.

I tried not to dwell on that. I referred to my Bible frequently throughout each day to keep my thoughts aligned. Carrying it with me to school required immense effort, but life was a constant battle of good versus evil, light versus darkness. I had to stay focused. Nothing could be more important than doing the Lord's work. It felt like a form of magic.

Every service at the Assembly of God involved casting out demons. Those seeking prayer and intervention would approach the front, forming a line. I always took an aisle seat near the back, hoping for dramatic displays of divine power—lightning bolts or thunderclaps. On slower days, I would return home feeling secretly disappointed.

The most faithful congregants gathered around anyone professing sickness or problems, laying hands on them as if channeling divine intervention through their palms.

"In the name of Jesus Christ, be gone, evil spirit of back pain!" Pastor Raeburn shouted, tapping a frail, elderly man on the forehead with the heel of his hand. "OUT IN THE NAME OF JESUS CHRIST OUR LORD! GET THEE BEHIND ME, SATAN!" he yelled.

I watched intently for any sign of an evil spirit, but all I saw was Mr. Gonzales, the frail, white-haired man, hobbling past the pews just as he had when he entered.

The congregation murmured "Amen," "Praise the Lord," and "Yes, Jesus!" as they waved their hands back and forth, whispering the lyrical tongues-speak in a chorus that lasted for twenty minutes or more. Mrs. Raeburn, the pastor's wife, provided musical accompaniment on the organ. Women—and a few men—shed ecstatic tears, while others shook with tremors, swaying from heel to toe with their eyes closed.

As I got older, the scene reminded me of a Grateful Dead concert, where everyone was on acid, but the clothes and music were entirely wrong.

I spoke in my spiritual language, lifting my palms toward heaven, though only to elbow height. I felt inhibited about exuberant public displays. Still, I practiced speaking in tongues at home, starting with a single consonant that flowed into random vowel sounds, letting it all meld together spontaneously.

My spiritual language took on a Spanish accent, not unlike the everyday speech of my friends at school.

A Soldier for Christ

1973

I was a soldier for Christ in a cataclysmic battle of good versus evil, but I had no idea what to do with my life after high school.

I was 14.

Mom frequently reminded me that I'd be expected to move out at 18 and I'd better have a job to support myself. "Your parents don't take care of you after you turn 18; you're on your own," she'd say, adding, "I was put to work in the slaughterhouse when I was eleven, so don't think you have it so bad."

Nobody in my family had ever gone to college. Finishing high school was considered a monumental achievement. Mom explained that if I didn't graduate, I could always take my GED test like she had. The GED was respectable enough. Yet, I'd never seen either of my parents crack open a book despite their investment in a set of encyclopedias when I was in first grade. Those encyclopedias were the only books in the house besides my own, and I often read them for fun. My parents were proud of my reading habit, hoping I would do better in life than they had.

From the time I was in second grade, Mom would drop me off at the library on Saturdays, returning an hour later to find me clutching a stack of books. Reading kept me out of her hair and became my refuge from sadness and loneliness.

My free time was largely spent at church or witnessing, trying to lead others to the Lord. At youth group, we were taught to be missionaries in our own neighborhoods. There was no need to travel to foreign countries when we were surrounded by Satan's prisoners right at home—everyone who didn't think like us. We bonded through fear; the devil was everywhere, even in our own families. Souls were ripe for harvesting in our homes and on our streets, and it was our job to bring them to God.

On Saturday nights, I'd watch the Billy Graham Crusades on the living room TV, hoping my father would pay attention to Billy's booming voice calling sinners to repent. It never worked; Dad lay on the couch, snoring through the broadcast no matter how loud I turned up the volume.

On summer days when school was out, it was all about witnessing. Candy and Denise were my youth group friends from the Assembly of God. Together, we trekked down dirty sidewalks strewn with cigarette butts, going door-to-door in our neighborhood, ringed by tall, skinny palm trees. Squinting in the smog-tinged yellow light of the California sun, we rang doorbells, sharing the gospel with indifferent neighbors. We offered a small booklet outlining the Three Easy Steps to Salvation and the chance to pray with us on the spot to be born again. Most neighbors were polite, but none accepted our offer.

Unlike the formally dressed Mormons or Jehovah's Witnesses who worked the same streets, we wore faded Levi's 501 jeans, ragged at the bottom, over our flip-flops. I sported a long copper French braid cascading down my back and favored gauzy, bohemian-style blouses that paired well with my denim jeans and flip-flops.

This was a significant departure from my peers, who might have been expected to sell Girl Scout cookies or magazine subscriptions. I was saving souls and thwarting the devil. How cool was that?

We packed Pop-Tarts for snacks or stopped by 7-11 for Snickers bars, sipping cold Pepsi from glass bottles.

At school, I was shy and soft-spoken, but when it came to witnessing for Jesus, I transformed into a holy warrior. Confident and relentless, I felt filled with the Spirit. I was battling God's arch-nemesis: Satan—Lucifer—Beelzebub—the Devil—who commanded an army of demons, leading humans straight to hell while tormenting Christians.

The big green leather-bound Living Bible I carried everywhere was my sword and shield, or so Pastor Raeburn had said. He was well-versed in these matters, and I watched closely to learn his techniques.

On a hot and dusty afternoon, my face flushed from the sun, I opened the front gate of Mrs. Peterson's white picket fence and climbed the steps to her shady front porch. The roses lining her walkway sweetened the air.

With my chest puffed out, I pressed the doorbell, feeling confident. Candy and Denise trailed behind, one on each side; they always let me do the talking.

I was good at making my case. My dad had joked that I should try selling vacuum cleaners or become a lawyer. I didn't find it funny, but then again, my dad wasn't a believer, so what did he know?

Mrs. Peterson knew me well. A friend of my grandmother's, she had bought candy and magazine subscriptions from me in the past when I rang her doorbell for school fundraisers.

I'd never witnessed to Mrs. Peterson about salvation before, but I expected it to go well; since she already liked me, I considered her an easy target.

"Hi, girls. What do you need today?" she smiled as she opened the door, her calf-length floral housedress swaying slightly. Her short white hair was permed tight, just like my grandma's.

"Hello, Mrs. Peterson! We're here to tell you about the Three Easy Steps to Salvation and how you, too, can have a personal relationship with Jesus Christ."

I pulled the small, illustrated tract from my back pocket and offered it to her. Mrs. Peterson's mouth puckered as she touched the booklet, her fingers stiffened by arthritis. She declined to take it.

"Oh honey, I've got that covered. I'm a member of the Episcopal Church. But thank you anyway. You girls, go on now and have a good day."

She stepped back, starting to close the door, but I placed my hand on the doorjamb and leaned in further.

"But Mrs. Peterson, I'm not talking about church membership. I'm talking about a real relationship with

Jesus and being filled with the Holy Spirit. The Episco-palians aren't filled with the Holy Spirit, which means they don't even know they're on the devil's side. They might be just one notch better than the Catholics, who aren't even Christians."

My gaze was steady. If the ground opened up right then and there, I feared Mrs. Peterson would be swal-lowed by the fires of hell. I didn't want that; I liked her.

Her lips formed a tight line. "I'm sorry, girls, I have a doctor's appointment. But wait right here a minute."

Candy and Denise looked hot and bored. They lacked motivation and weren't the best at fighting Satan; I figured they wouldn't even go witnessing without me leading the way.

Mrs. Peterson returned with a small crystal bowl filled with M&Ms. "Here, girls. Have some candy before you go," she said, smiling as she thrust the bowl toward us.

We each took a handful of M&Ms and then turned to walk back down the sidewalk, our flip-flops flapping against the scorching asphalt, which was so hot it was beginning to soften and melt.

The Dirty Boulevard

1973

They called him Lurch, though everyone in school knew his given name was Richard. You only had to glance to understand why. Close to seven feet tall with a big square head, Lurch was a twenty-something smack addict known to be a ruthless drug dealer. He had dirty blonde hair and dead yellow-green eyes.

Lurch became my curse when I was in 9th grade.

Every day, I walked a perilous three miles to and from school down the boulevard, the main thoroughfare through town. The dilapidated duplex where Lurch lived was across the street from the Chevron station, just past the 7-11, where I stopped to get a slurpy if I could find enough quarters in my pocket on hot days.

Lurch tended to hang out in the front yard when school let out at 2:45. On a good day, he would stand on the thin brown lawn tinkering with the rusted-out metal husk of a broken-down red Camero and stare at me as I walked by. He never gestured or said a word, just that long, fixed gaze that followed me with a flat, reptilian stare.

I learned to pretend to ignore him and walked purposefully, keeping my pace steady and eyes fixed on the horizon before me; despite my nonchalant appearance, my muscles felt spring loaded, and I prayed silently. "God, please keep him away from me." I already knew that it was critically important to show no fear, though I was filled with it. People like Lurch fed off fear.

On good days, I passed him right by, and nothing happened. On a bad day, Lurch would up the ante.

Once a week or so, he'd skulk to the sidewalk when he saw me coming, taking a stance directly where I had to pass; facing me, he'd stand right in the middle of the walkway, effectively blocking the path of my 5'4" slender body with his bulk.

Lurch loomed over me. If I tried to get around him by stepping to the right, he'd step to that side, too. He'd do the same when I tried to step to the left. If I wanted to pass, I was at his mercy. First right, then left, and then stuck in the middle again. Lurch was in total control of the dance and never said a word. Though my heart thumped, neither did I.

I kept my face expressionless and never made eye contact. Lurch never tried to touch me, but he let me know he could—and there would be nothing I could do about it if he did. I knew that, too. But I knew he wanted to scare me, and though he did, I wouldn't let him know it.

The silent right and left dance could go on for minutes, eventually ending when other pedestrians approached on the sidewalk. Then, wordless, he'd step to the side, and I'd soldier on, never looking back. I was never hurt—it was just another walk home from school. Nonetheless, his malevolence took a bite out of my spirit.

It was common on the boulevard for men in cars to pull over and offer me rides home. Sometimes, they were older boys I recognized from high school, but often, they were adult men, too. If they didn't look too sketchy, I'd take them up on the offer. It beat walking past Lurch.

Occasionally, a chopper would roar up behind me, and one of several large, bearded men with long hair named Bear, or Mooch, or Spider would say, "Hey, Red, Wanna ride?" The motorcycle guys usually wore denim vests with green and red VAGOS motorcycle club logos on the back.

They may have been notorious, but they were always polite to me. When they asked for my phone number, I intentionally scrambled the digits.

Three years after high school, Lurch was arrested for murdering two 16-year-olds who'd stolen two kilos of marijuana from him. The boys were both shot in the head and left in the dirt outside the Blue Bird Mobile Home Park nearby. One of them scrawled the letters "l-u-r-c-h" on the ground with his bloody finger as he lay dying.

Grandma Always Said

1974

Grandma always said it was best to wait until you graduated high school before you got married.

But then she'd recite the list of female cousins back in Kansas who had not waited. Linda, Jean, Sue, Shirley —they'd all been 16. "The law requires that much now," she said as if this indicated progress.

Grandma hadn't mentioned that she had just been 14, and my mother was barely 13 when they married for the first time. And she indeed never confided that they'd both been raped by men more than twice their age and impregnated before their shotgun weddings in rural Oklahoma and Kansas, respectively.

Weddings without white dresses and flowers. Weddings at the courthouse, not the church. Little girls dressed up as shamed pregnant brides on their way to lives of abuse and violence as uneducated dirt-poor farm wives who would be serially pregnant but eventually divorced and remarried to better men.

As a kid, I asked a lot of questions, but I never got straight answers—like why I had two half-brothers and a half-sister already in their twenties by the time I was born. Why did we never talk about the fact that they had different last names and a different father? They felt more like uncles and an aunt than siblings. It was always awkward to explain why my nieces and nephews were the same age as me, so we just called each other cousins. I begged for a brother or sister closer to my age, but Mom would only give me a hard, angry look.

When I was in middle school, fantasizing about getting married in a long white dress with a flowing train, I asked my mother if I could see her wedding dress. I imagined it carefully packed away in a closet, like my friend Shelly's mom's.

"I wore a blue suit," she said curtly. "Me and your dad got married at the courthouse. There aren't any pictures." Her tone was sharp, cutting off the conversation.

I often felt like I was trying to piece together a puzzle with half the pieces missing. Nothing made sense. Dots never connected. The gaps were enormous, and though I couldn't fully understand, I knew we were different from other families in Southern California. It wasn't just the backwoods way they spoke.

A few years later, my mother would finally reveal that when she was 12, she'd buried a baby under a yellow rose bush after her sister's self-induced, nearly full-term abortion.

Dark threads seemed to weave through every family

story, just below the surface. There were reasons for the silence, but it would take years before I understood them—long after I'd already absorbed patterns I didn't yet comprehend.

Matrimony

1976–1980s

I met my first husband at the Assembly of God church on a Saturday night when the Christian rock bands played. I was fifteen.

Greg was a towering figure, proudly self-identified as Mexican and Native American, and newly born-again. He worked as an electrician, was a decade older than me, and had recently left behind his part-time gig selling weed. When he invited me for a ride on his motorcycle, I couldn't help but admire how his long black hair flew behind him as we sped off on his Harley-Davidson, unencumbered by helmets.

Of course, we prayed together, and he'd pick me up for church on the motorcycle. After a month, I found myself with him whenever he wasn't working or I wasn't in school. He took me along for errands—grocery shopping, trips to the auto parts store—and I savored the meals he cooked. I often slept over at his house, rarely seeing my parents. I felt like a fully functioning adult, and I'm not even sure they noticed I was gone.

Having grown up with emotional deprivation, isolation, and self-hatred, being with a man who wanted to spend time with me felt soothing. Greg would take care of me.

I'd never attended a high school dance or prom, but Greg assured me it was God's will for us to marry, and who was I to argue with God?

"Well, we'd better hurry up then," I said because we've already had sex, and that's a serious sin." I felt tormented by guilt about that and would be relieved to be married.

Greg bought me an engagement ring I had picked out at Zale's Jewelers in the mall. It was a thin white gold band with a tiny solitary diamond. As soon as we set the date, I started using his last name as my own. Despite practically living together, the official ceremony still took another year. Since I was under 18, I had to get permission from the court which took a lot of paperwork and a meeting with a social worker. He decided after 30 minutes I was mature enough to marry.

We had a small church wedding on a Saturday night during my senior year of high school. I wore a Gunne Sak dress and carried a delicate bouquet of yellow daisies.

Though I had invited friends from school, none came. The only attendees were my immediate family and a handful of church acquaintances. By then, my few high school friends had distanced themselves from me, which stung because I couldn't understand why. Yet, despite the absence of friends, I felt a profound relief to belong to someone and proudly wore my wedding ring when I returned to school on Monday.

I loved it when Greg picked me up from school on the Harley. The rude jocks who grabbed my butt in the hallways moved aside as we thundered past them in front of the campus. Greg made me feel safe; nobody would dare mess with me now, not even Lurch. He was a powerful man, unafraid of anyone.

Becoming a godly housewife and mother seemed to solve my post-high school dilemma. Greg would support me, and I could have kids. I envisioned myself as a perfect mother, committed to raising flawless children. I vowed never to yell or raise a hand in anger at them and would be very different from my mother. I was determined to get this mothering thing right.

Greg taught me practical skills like writing a check, making Mexican food, and changing the vacuum cleaner bag. He even helped me with algebra homework and called the attendance office to excuse my sick days.

Firm believers in the power of prayer, we prayed aloud together. Much like Pastor Raeburn, Greg had a palpable fear of Satan and often spoke of sensing demons lurking nearby. Though he was fatherly, he wasn't demonstrative; words of affection were scarce. Our intimacy felt cold and mechanical, and he never held my hand.

Greg made a good living at the steel mill, and when I discovered I was pregnant just five weeks after our wedding, we sold his Harley for five thousand dollars. This gave us a down payment on an old white farm-style house, only fifteen feet from the train tracks in a sketchy part of town.

The freight train thundered through precisely at 2:00 every afternoon and again at 10:00 at night, shaking the entire house and rattling the floors. You had to stop talking whenever the train passed because it drowned out everything.

If you left your car parked on the street, the local gangs would tag it with black spray paint. Tall, skinny palm trees lined both sides of our street, and large white screech owls nested in their tops. At night, when the Sheriff's helicopter thumped rhythmically overhead, surveilling the block, its giant spotlight illuminated the big white birds, sending them screeching in frantic circles around the trees.

Blood

1976

In that neighborhood, I learned that blood has a stench in large quantities. It goes with violent death, and the smell can linger forever.

Bill and Trisha, an emaciated and scabby married couple in their mid-30s, lived next door in a weathered one-bedroom duplex. For the most part, they kept to themselves. Every evening around 10:00, the sound of Bill's yelling and Trisha's crying carried through the neighborhood. It became background noise that the rest of the residents on the block learned to filter out.

When I was six months pregnant, I sat on my back porch stairs under a canopy of stars, trying to catch a cool breeze. Bill was shouting like usual, but I couldn't make out his words. Suddenly, a gunshot blasted a hole in the air, followed immediately by shattering female screams. My dog started barking and running back and forth along the fence line. My first thought was, "Oh my God, he's trying to kill her."

Reflexively, I ran barefoot toward the sound from the duplex, jumping the low chain link fence, pregnant belly and all. I didn't pause to consider what I was doing.

The wooden front door was open; I could see through the screen. Trisha sat on the floor with Bill's bloody head cradled in her lap, and his legs stretched out in front of them. A chunk of his skull was missing, and blood plastered his shirt to his chest. He took great heaving, rattling breaths. Realizing this was awful, I felt stymied on how to help. A strange, awful smell filled the room.

Hugging Bill to her, Trisha kept shrieking, barely registering my presence when I called her name. A black handgun was next to him on the floor, along with muddy gray flecks of brain.

I ran back outside and shouted for Greg, who appeared at our front door under the porch-light but didn't come over himself. "He's shot—call 911!" I yelled. Greg turned and disappeared back inside.

"Why, oh my god, why?" Trisha wailed, looking up at me when I ran in. "Get a blanket; we need to cover him so he doesn't go into shock!" she gasped, her breaths coming short and fast. I had a feeling it was too late to worry about Bill going into shock, but I ran to get a blanket from their bed and lay it over him as his chest alternately rose and then collapsed, with great heaving breaths.

The police and EMTs arrived within five minutes. There was a flurry of action in the small living room as they positioned Bill on a stretcher and tried to start an IV. "These veins are all collapsed," a younger EMT said, probing his arms and then his neck. "He's got sclerosis

—this is going to be a struggle."

Two police officers surveyed the household and asked questions. "Whose needles are these?" the older one asked Trisha, gesturing to the hypodermic syringes on the coffee table.

"They're ours," she said, her voice breaking. "It's heroin and crystal." Holding up her bloody palms in front of her, she looked down at them and started retching. I thought she was going to vomit.

When the cop stepped away, I took Trisha's elbow and guided her into the bathroom to help her wash the blood off her hands. Her sweatpants and t-shirt were soaked red with clinging bits of gray tissue. "Try to breathe slowly," I said, "let's pray for a miracle."

With my hand on her shoulder, I said, "Lord Jesus, we ask you to heal Bill. Please send your spirit to him now. Bless and comfort Trisha, Lord. Surround her with your angels and bring her peace. In your holy name, amen."

When the policeman noticed what we were doing, he yelled at me. "Girl, you're interfering with an investigation. She's a suspect here. Stay away from her, and don't wash anything off until we get photographs. She's going with me down to the station."

"You're cruel," I said, incensed. In my mind, it was clear that Bill had shot himself.

Trisha was trembling and sobbing as the police questioned her. Yes, Bill had a history of violence; he had a temper. That night, they'd been arguing when he grabbed the handgun out of the drawer in the living room end table and, looking her straight in the eyes, shot himself in the temple.

Bill died in the ambulance. Trisha never returned to their home, though she wasn't criminally charged. For years afterward, whenever I caught sight of the duplex out of the corner of my eye, the distinct metallic stench of blood would come flooding back into my nostrils. The smell reminded me of raw meat and made me nauseous. No matter how hard I tried to banish the odor, it never went away.

Combustion

1977–80

I had always gotten good grades in school and even graduated a semester early. But I skipped my high school graduation ceremony and the Grad Night celebration at Disneyland. My belly was as big as a Volkswagen Bug, and Greg definitely wouldn't have fit in with the crowd.

The following year, Grandma dropped dead from a heart attack in her kitchen—just like Grandpa had. One minute she was there, the next she was gone. Her house sat empty, and the geraniums and violets she'd so carefully tended in the flower beds began to wither. It made me sad to watch them die, like the house itself was grieving.

A few years later, my dad let my 30-year-old cousin Mitch move into Grandma's cottage. Mitch had lost his job and apartment—again. He was chronically underfunctioning but blonde and good-looking, with a wide, charming grin that made people want to take a chance on him. Dad charged him $150 a month in rent, and Mitch promised to be quiet and cause no trouble.

Mitch was known for substance abuse and terrible judgment. At the time, he was sleeping with a married woman, Chelsea—who, unfortunately, was married to Phat Jack, a petty criminal I'd gone to high school with. Jack had a shaved head and arms covered in crude, black self-inflicted tattoos.

Phat Jack wasn't the type to let infidelity slide. Late one Saturday night, he poured gasoline around the outside of Grandma's house and set it on fire while Mitch and Chelsea were inside, asleep. They barely escaped through the bedroom window. The fire gutted the cottage, though it could've been worse if it hadn't been built of cinderblock. Phat Jack was convicted of arson and sent to prison.

Dad wasn't fazed. He drove the bulldozer himself to tear down what was left of the house and hauled away the wreckage. "It don't matter none," he said. "Nobody's gonna try moving in there now. One less problem for me to deal with."

A year later, Mitch died alone of a heroin overdose.

No one was surprised.

The Missing

1930s–1970s

The missing children were critical threads woven into my family's intricate tapestry of secrets. Some had names, while others faded into obscurity. When names were remembered, they were often forgotten again—deliberately. Forgetting was a pattern my family excelled at.

After my marriage, my mother became a frequent evening visitor, often stopping by on her way home from work. Greg worked the swing shift at the steel mill, leaving me alone during evening hours. Mom would often pick up a small gift for my unborn child from Kmart before arriving, a gesture that seemed to bridge the gulf between us. We had navigated a stressful childhood and my volatile teenage years, but now, with a baby on the way, we finally had something joyful to share.

I spent my days engrossed in Lamaze books, confident that enough prayer and preparation would allow me to master a pain-free childbirth. I quickly accumulated a small library on natural birth, breastfeeding, and child-rearing, and in typical fashion, prematurely deemed myself an expert. At sixteen, pregnancy and motherhood dominated my conversations. While my peers were absorbed in high school life, I had charted a course of my own and was feeling a rare sense of closeness to my mother. The weight of childrearing had shifted from her to me, and for the first time, I felt her love most clearly—albeit from a comfortable distance. She loved me best that way.

I busied myself preparing the perfect nest: adopting a collie dog, buying a second-hand crib from a garage sale, and making a half-hearted attempt at starting a vegetable garden. We installed orange shag carpet in our old farmhouse, oblivious to how it clashed with the architecture.

I developed strong opinions about nearly everything. In line with my religion, I was fiercely opposed to abortion—a topic that dominated the news after Roe v. Wade. I could be judgmental, arrogant, and self-righteous—your typical prickly teenager.

"Remember Eileen from high school?" I asked one evening as my mother and I sipped iced tea, the twilight softly settling in through the living room windows. "She had an abortion last week. There's no excuse for that—she could've put the baby up for adoption."

A long silence followed as Mom gazed toward the corner of the room, her expression distant. When she finally spoke, her voice softened, hesitant. "I know something about abortion," she began, her words measured. "It's complicated. Women can get desperate."

My heart skipped. Conversations about personal matters were foreign ground for her, and hearing her tread this unfamiliar territory made me feel unsettled. In that brief, unexpected moment of vulnerability, the armor she always wore cracked, if only slightly.

At 51, my mother didn't know that a malignant tumor had already begun its quiet invasion deep within her brain. If I had known we had only weeks left to connect as adults, I would have clung to every word, eager to unearth the history we so carefully avoided. But I wasn't practiced in deep conversations, especially not with her. So, I just sat there, frozen, listening.

Mom rarely spoke about her past. She and her four siblings grew up on a small farm in rural Kansas. Their house, built of rock, lacked indoor plumbing, and heat came from a wood stove. They relied on an old wooden outhouse and pumped water from a well. The girls stitched their dresses from floral fabric scavenged from flour sacks, saving for months to collect enough material for just one dress.

I had heard many stories about the hardships of farm life during the Great Depression, but my mother never shared personal details about relationships or emotions. She avoided the darker subjects—pain, fear, and grief.

But that evening, something shifted. In a voice that didn't seem like her own, she stared out the window at the newly lit streetlight and began to reveal the story of Helen, her secret sister.

"Grandma always said she had five children. And she did—with Grandpa: four girls and one boy. But there was another marriage before Grandpa, to a man she married when she was still a girl. The daughter from that marriage was named Helen."

The first part of the secret was that grandma had been married at 14, to a 31-year-old named Charles—a union far from voluntary. A few months later, she gave birth to Helen on the Caddo reservation in Oklahoma, where they lived and farmed. The 1911 census recorded my grandmother as a housewife, married to Charles, a farmer, both residing in his mother's home.

Two years later, census records show a dramatic change: Grandma had relocated to Kansas, now married to my grandfather, Thomas, with a new baby girl named Annie. Helen, meanwhile, had been left behind in Oklahoma, with Charles and his mother. She would grow up there, separated from the rest of the family.

Charles was erased from my grandmother's history; no one ever spoke of him again. Most of her family didn't even know that he—or Helen—had existed.

My mother met her half-sister for the first time when she was twelve and Helen was twenty. "Helen showed up at our farm in Kansas," Mom recalled. "None of us kids knew who she was. She was eight months pregnant and unmarried. She came looking for help."

Helen didn't receive a warm welcome. Like Ida, she was seen as "not right in the head," and her odd behavior was interpreted as stubbornness. "Helen wouldn't get out of bed; she didn't help with anything. She had no way to care for a child," Mom said, her voice tense with memory.

"Grandma told her she'd have to put the baby up for adoption, and Helen didn't like that. They had a bad ruckus." Mom paused, taking a shaky breath.

"Two days later, Helen found an old woman veterinarian in town to help her induce an abortion. The vet broke her water with a knitting needle and gave her some herbs. Then Helen walked back to the farm to labor in secret. She shared a bedroom with Ida and me, so I knew what was happening. When the pain became too much, she went to the outhouse and pushed the baby out into the toilet. She didn't know if it was born dead or alive."

A chill ran through me. My skin prickled as I instinctively cradled my own belly, nausea rising. Suddenly, the room around me felt disorienting, the angles too sharp, too wrong.

"The next day, Grandma figured out what Helen had done. She was furious—screaming. Not only had Helen committed a crime, but now there was a baby in the pit beneath the outhouse. Grandma wouldn't abide that."

With my grandfather working in the fields, Grandma ordered my mother and her siblings to move the heavy outhouse off the pit—a monumental task for the children.

"It was so hot," Mom recalled. "The older girls complained, but you couldn't argue with Grandma."

She described sifting through the filth with garden rakes under the blistering Kansas sun, searching for the baby's body. It took half the morning.

Ida, the youngest at just nine years old, was tasked with washing the tiny body in an enamel basin to prepare it for burial. Afterward, my mother dressed the baby in a pink doll's dress, placed her gently in a shoebox, and buried her beneath a yellow rose bush in the yard.

"It was a tiny, perfect baby girl," she said softly, tears gathering in the corners of her eyes. That was the closest I ever came to seeing my mother cry. I've always thought that if she'd ever shed a single tear, she would have drowned.

"Grandma ran Helen off that day," my mother continued, her voice steadier now. "We never heard from her again. I don't know the whole story, but sometimes I think... maybe an early abortion would have been the kinder choice for everyone involved."

❧ ❧ ❧

Decades later, with the help of online DNA services, I tracked down six mysterious cousins from Idaho to Oklahoma, all of them Helen's children. She had raised none; all were adoptees. Helen led a transient life and never married.

Years later, a distant cousin would explain that during Ida's time in the mental hospital, she rambled about dead babies to anyone who would listen.

The story of Helen left my gut churning. Grandma was gone, and Mom must have finally felt free to share the tale. I hugged her gently when she left that evening but couldn't find any words that seemed right. I was only beginning to grasp the sources of the turbulence within her, but there would be no more deep conversations. In just a few short months, without warning, she would slip into a coma.

Howling

1977–1980s

I had been howling like a suffering animal for 20 straight hours; my voice was hoarse, and my heartbeat hammered in my ears. With a dry mouth and lips split, I was ready to die. "Please, just shoot me if you can't get this baby out!" I yelled at the obstetrician. "Someone give me a gun! I do not want to do this anymore!"

While the contractions made my abdomen rock hard, the worst pain was in my lower back. The muscles twisted tighter and tighter and nothing I did helped the pain. My body had never been so out of control before, and I thrashed around the bed in the room that smelled like disinfectant.

It was not supposed to go this way. I'd taken Lamaze classes, practiced Kegels every time I peed, ate healthy (mostly), exercised, and most importantly—I'd prayed to be delivered from the pain of childbirth. I had faith and had boasted to my friends that I'd have an entirely natural and pain-free birth, but clearly, it wasn't working out that way. Since I'd told the doctor when I arrived that I wanted a natural birth, there was no anesthesiologist available to provide an epidural when I had changed my mind.

I was a teenager married to a 26-year-old man.

I lay on the hospital bed with the IV needle stuck in the back of my hand; the fluorescent lights hurt my eyes, and the air smelled medicinal. My hair and the flimsy hospital gown were soaked with sweat; doctors and nurses kept spreading my legs and sticking their hands up my vagina to check my cervix, which was refusing to open. The labor pain was like nothing I'd ever experienced; there were no breaks between contractions, and after 20 hours, I was still barely dilated. It was clear to me that this whole baby thing had been a terrible idea, and God wasn't helping one bit. My faith had failed me.

"I'll take a C-section—just put me out! I don't care anymore!" I yelled. So much for relaxation breathing and a focal point, I felt betrayed by God and the Lamaze teachers. This wasn't what I'd been promised.

Not to mention, Greg made a lousy birth coach. He kept falling asleep despite my screaming. His somnolence was the only genuinely miraculous thing in evidence that night. "If I can't sleep, you can't sleep either!" I yelled. Despite this, his eyes closed, and his head drooped forward; I was pissed.

But prayer wasn't helping one bit with the labor pain. Neither was it curing the depression that had become an all-encompassing gray cloud over my life, which I couldn't pray away.

After 24 hours of hard labor and an aggressive

Pitocin drip, I gave birth to a son, a perfectly healthy eight-pound boy. I went home a few hours after his birth and mopped the floor. While the labor had been hell, the recovery afterward was near instantaneous. My young body bounced back immediately.

I would go on to have two more babies—a girl and another boy—In the coming six years as I tried to mold myself into a godly stay-at-home wife and mother. When my same-age friends from high school were off at college and attending parties and nightclubs, I spent time at La Leche League, childbirth classes, and women's Bible studies with women a decade or two older than me. I had a template for my life. I breastfed each baby for a year and fed them healthy, organic, carefully chosen foods.

A sticky note on my bedroom mirror read, "The only reason I'm alive is to serve God in all I do."

In truth, I thought a lot about death and had trouble getting out of bed. I stayed alive because I loved my children and swore to be a perfect mother—and I've always been one to keep my commitments.

Rise Up and Walk

1978

The year after my first son's birth, my mother lay comatose in a rented hospital bed in the living room of the family home. Dying of an inoperable brain tumor, she was as still as a corpse and had been in that condition for six months.

I nursed my baby while caring for her. My father and I had to shift her body every two hours to prevent bed sores. We were religious about it.

Desperate, I turned to God again. If he could raise Lazarus from the tomb and heal lepers, he could undoubtedly heal my mother. I believed in miracles.

I stood over her body, pale as wax, and held her limp hand while I pleaded with God to heal her. Day after day, nothing happened. I felt tears well up, but I couldn't let them leak out of my eyes.

Like most people in my church, I watched the Christian television show The 700 Club, featuring televangelist Pat Robertson. Pat was fiery and, just like Pastor Raeburn, focused on the devil as much as he did Jesus. Pat preached miraculous healing and promised sick viewers that God would heal the faithful who prayed. He conducted faith healings on the air and had a team of prayer warriors manning hotlines that you could see in the background during the broadcasts. They promised miracles just before the segment when Pat begged for monthly donations.

I sat next to my mother's bed on a Sunday night, watching The 700 Club. Halfway into the program, I impulsively went into the kitchen, picked up the phone, and dialed the 800 number for the prayer request hotline.

"700 Club Prayer Hotline," a woman's voice said. "God bless you. How can we help you?"

My voice trembled. "My mother is in a coma. She's dying from a brain tumor. We're praying that she will be healed. I'm asking for prayer."

"Of course, honey, raise your hands to the Lord and pray with me right now." Her voice became louder. "Lord Jesus, in your name, we banish the spirit of disease from this sister—heal her now as she's filled with your spirit. Let this sister rise up and walk! By the blood of the lamb, may it be done! We claim this. She shall rise up and walk. In your blessed name, amen."

"Amen," I said.

"Honey, go to your mother and tell her to rise up and walk. She is healed. Thank you for calling the 700 Club."

It seemed so easy, and I couldn't help feeling suspicious as I thanked her and hung up, but I tried to swallow my doubt. If I didn't have faith, it wouldn't work. I had to make myself believe.

Walking back to the bedside, I looked at her still face and couldn't bring myself to say the magic words aloud. But knowing that God hears our thoughts, I figured that saying it in my mind should work.

Come on, Mom. In Jesus' name, rise up and walk.

I repeated the magic words three times, but there was not so much as a flutter of her pale, thin eyelids; something in me deflated. It was getting harder and harder to have faith.

Prayer didn't save me from the pain of childbirth; prayer didn't heal my mother. Neither did prayer heal my baby's ear infection—that took antibiotics from the doctor. I watched a child from the Assembly of God die of leukemia despite months of prayer and the casting out of demons. My beliefs were starting to crumble, and I struggled to make sense of things.

After nine months, my mother died quietly at home with my father and me at her bedside; the next day, I broke out in a bright red rash all over my body. It would persist for months.

The Willow Tree

1970s–1980s

Two years before her brain grew cancerous, my mother planted a weeping willow tree in the backyard. She took good care of it. Fertilized and watered regularly, its slender trunk and wispy limbs grew solid and tall.

On the day of Mom's death, Aunt Annie hugged me to her bosom as she sobbed. "It was the willow tree that did this. I told her not to plant it."

"What do you mean?" I asked, perplexed. "I think the tree is beautiful, and she loved it."

"Child, this is something I've known since I was your age," she said. "If you plant a willow tree, you'll die when it grows big enough to cover your grave. I warned your mama. We should cut the damn thing down before someone else goes."

She said the same thing to my father, who only rolled his eyes. The tree stayed.

A decade and a half later, my father remarried, and my stepmother, who was 50 and a drinker, died shortly after that of cirrhosis, a disease none of us knew she had.

I didn't blame the tree. I couldn't help but wonder if there wasn't something about my father that sucked the life out of women.

The Middle Kingdom

1983

Five years after my mother's death, the steel mill closed, and Greg was laid off. Desperate to move away from the Inland Empire, I urged him to look to the northern part of the state for work. I typed up his resumes and mailed them to industrial plants and utility companies in beautiful locations where I dreamed of living.

He was eventually hired at the nuclear power plant on the Central Coast of California. Six months later, we moved 250 miles north with a little boy, a toddler, and a newborn. We settled in a small town on the ocean.

The Central Coast was a land of strawberry fields and orange poppies. Monterrey pines and rugged cliffs hugged the sea. Otters floated on their backs in the bays, sea lions reclined on the shores, and fish and chip restaurants and farmer's markets were plentiful.

Though my new home was on a dead-end dirt road, it still felt like the promised land. I could hear the sound of the ocean just a few blocks away.

For the first time in my life, I could expand my lungs down to my belly. The sea mist softened the light and turned my hair curly.

When you're not used to clean air, you never take it for granted. I wanted my kids to grow up under blue skies. I rejoiced in escaping the Inland Empire, its crime, and graffiti. I wanted my kids to walk to school without drug dealers, gangs, and outlaw motorcycle gangs as ever-present companions.

Greg found a church with a young, charismatic surfer as a pastor. He didn't trumpet from the pulpit, and the faith-healing rhetoric was toned down. Nonetheless, I attended without enthusiasm and was always itching for a reason to leave. Greg held his faith closely, but I held my doubts closer.

I read voraciously, bringing home stacks of books on child development and popular psychology from the library. I felt like I was mapping reality for the first time. Desperate for something to occupy my mind, I became a self-taught Lamaze childbirth instructor at 23 years old —though in my classes, which were mostly populated by women from my church, I emphasized that there was no guarantee that the birth would be pain-free. I became an advocate for lay midwifery after giving birth to my third child at home, which was a much easier experience than my previous hospital births.

Nonetheless, my melancholia lingered. My life was a too-tight shoe.

Greg worked 12-hour shifts at the nuclear plant and

left all aspects of child-rearing to me. Since he was assigned to the graveyard shift, he slept during the day, and I had to work hard to keep the kids quiet.

Greg was cold and judgmental, just like God. His voice was perpetually displeased. Since he was the breadwinner, he considered all the money his. I had to ask permission before buying anything.

"I'd like to order pizza for the kids tonight," I'd say on a typical Saturday.

"We can't spend money on frivolous things," he responded, though he bought himself an aluminum bass boat and expensive photography equipment he never had time to use.

I felt like his child and resented him.

Though he never raged, his was a quiet anger. I was starting to imagine what life would be like apart from him.

In my nightmares, he was trying to kill me.

PART III

"You might as well answer the door, my child,
the truth is furiously knocking."

Lucille Clifton
THE LIONESS AWAKENS

Therapy

1983–1986

I sat in the tan leather armchair, nursing my third baby with a flannel blanket discreetly tucked around his head to cover my breast. I had no one to watch him while I went to therapy, so I took the baby with me. Gazing down at him, I struggled to describe my emotions. I wasn't good at it. I'd never learned a language for my own feelings.

You don't always have a hit with the first therapist you try. It was therapist number three for the win. Her name was Rosalyn.

I'd tried two others first: an awkward older man with thick glasses who played jazz music in his waiting room and couldn't relate to me, followed by a single visit with a terse helmet-haired woman who was cold and distant. I felt uncomfortable with both and mostly sat silently for the two single 50-minute hours. I had no idea what to discuss, and they apparently didn't know what questions to ask.

I understood that my malaise, hopelessness, and leaden extremities were symptoms of depression. I'd tried to pray it away for years to no avail. I was willing to give therapy one more try because I was desperate.

Rosalyn was different. There was a click between us, and she touched something profound inside me. With a lilting Australian accent, she was in her early 30s and so warm that I felt a radiance just sitting in her office. Something within me melted around her.

"So, tell me more about what God is like for you," Rosalyn said the spring morning of our second visit after I'd explained how much I'd gone to church. "Is he really this mean old man that lives in your head, reminding you how awful you are all the time? I know what this is like because my father is a minister back in Australia. I grew up hearing that every single thing about me was sinful, and he never let me forget it."

"That's exactly how it is," I said. "No matter how hard I try, a voice in my head tells me I'm never good enough."

"And when you notice that, how do you feel?" she asked.

I took a moment to ponder. "Depressed," I said. "And I'm not supposed to be depressed. The Bible says I should be joyful. Which makes me more depressed and guilty—I feel guilty."

That's exactly how it works, " she said, " and we're going to throw all that right out the window while you're in this office. There is no guilt present here. All thoughts and feelings are welcome—except guilt."

"You need to learn to express your emotions. You've locked them up before you even know that they're there. You're good at saying what you think but not what you feel," she said. "But that doesn't make them go away— all that pressure from holding your feelings in makes you miserable."

My sense of shame lifted after talking to Rosalyn, but I often felt unsteady walking out of her office. Things inside shifted after our conversations, sometimes making the room spin. It was as if gears began clicking into new places in my head.

There were light flashes as I began to speak my feelings about Greg.

"He's more like a father than a husband," I told her. If I met him now, I wouldn't even date him." I was tired of church and his talk about Satan. We shared nothing in common other than the children, and he spent next to no time with any of us.

I felt stifled and wanted to do something with my life beyond just mothering, but I had no idea what was possible.

She leaned toward me and softened her voice. "You're capable of more than you think you are. Going to church is a choice. What you believe about spirituality is a choice. And being married to Greg is a choice. You are not without power here. You are young—it's not too late to go to college and have a career if you should choose to."

"Choice" was the scariest word anyone had ever said to me.

Education

1983–1989

At 23, I sat in a sunlit community college classroom, wearing tan Birkenstocks and a knee-length denim skirt. My copper hair was woven into a long French braid, and the sunscreen I applied faithfully had allowed my freckles to fade. As I took notes on a yellow spiral pad, my gray-haired Jungian professor paced at the front of the room.

"If the devil is knocking at your door, open up and let him in," the professor said. "He's got something to tell you about yourself. Satan is nothing but a projection of our own shadow; there's no devil other than us walking about the earth."

I was spellbound, hanging on to his every word.

Surprisingly, I was excelling in college, something I never expected. I had always believed I wasn't made for higher education, but I was earning straight A's so far, though that pattern would change when I got to math classes. Initially, I signed up for every psychology class available, each one opening new perspective for me. Psychology helped me make sense of the world and the people around me, igniting a small beacon of hope. For the first time, I found answers to my questions. If I could understand people, I thought, maybe I could make life work out.

I had abandoned thoughts of the devil and the punitive God who once haunted my mind, and I stopped going to church. This only deepened the tension between Greg and me. "You're not following God's word," he would say grimly.

"I don't think we see the world the same way," I'd respond, feeling the distance grow. "I've changed. I'm not 15 anymore."

I also repeatedly told Greg I wasn't sure I wanted to stay married. But Greg, never one to listen, pretended not to hear me.

꽃 꽃 꽃

Life became a balancing act. Fueled by stress and sheer determination, I juggled school, childcare, grocery shopping, and keeping the kids entertained. I was determined to finish my degree quickly, at least in less than five years. The house was a constant mess, and the divide between Greg and me grew wider. The kids learned early how to make their own sandwiches and use the microwave, but I didn't have time to feel guilty about it—I was focused on getting an education.

For the next four years, I drove a beige Volkswagen Squareback, with baby seats in the back, to classes where I studied human behavior and how not to screw up my kids. The car was always messy—rumpled toddler clothes and cracker crumbs covered the floor. But I kept at it.

Eventually, I earned my bachelor's degree in psychology, and my thinking shifted again. I began seeing possibilities I had never considered before. Six months after graduation, I got a job and told Greg I was filing for divorce.

My first job was at a residential treatment home for people with schizophrenia. The pay was minimal, but I found the work deeply fulfilling. The clients—people dealing with hallucinations and delusions—felt like family to me.

The agency housed eight residents in a large Victorian home, none of whom could live independently. A small staff team rotated shifts, providing 24-hour care. We acted as companions, helped with chores, organized shopping, managed their Social Security benefits, and worked on coping mechanisms. My title was Residential Treatment Counselor.

One resident, a petite blonde woman in her 20s, whom I'll call Susan, reminded me of my Aunt Ida, sharing the same distant look in her eyes. One night, angry at the voices in her head, Susan threw a chair in her bedroom, leaving a large hole in the drywall next to her bed. Fearing she'd be in trouble, Susan decided to patch the hole with a frozen chicken from the freezer. I discovered the chicken the next morning as I supervised chores.

We didn't reprimand her—if anything, it was a creative solution—but I called the handyman for a more permanent fix than the thawed chicken wedged in the wall.

Among the residents was a man I'll call John, a towering figure in his 40s with severe bipolar disorder. He was also a gifted pianist and composer. During his manic episodes, which could last for weeks, he'd stop sleeping and begin seeing and hearing things that weren't there.

When manic, John believed he was married to Whitney Houston despite never having met her. This delusion grew problematic when he tried to hitchhike to LA to find her. He was stranded 90 miles away in Santa Barbara after his ride abandoned him on the freeway. The police called us, and it became my job to pick him up and bring him back home.

John also believed he was running for President. On the drive back, we stopped at a Denny's, where he decided to hold an impromptu campaign event. He went from table to table, shaking hands and introducing himself. "Hello, I'm John, and I'm running for President. I'd appreciate your vote."

I explained the situation to the manager, who was gracious and played along, telling John he had just missed the right day for campaigning but was welcome to try again. We got our food to go and ate in the car on the way back.

John had frequent run-ins with the police and was a regular at the county psychiatric ward. Despite his troubles, I liked him a lot. He reminded me of an uncle who was always in and out of jail.

My job was to help clients recognize patterns in their symptoms, stay on their medications, and develop a system of mental checks and balances to avoid being hospitalized. The work felt so natural that it was surprising to me that I was being paid for it. But I realized I could do more if I kept studying, I could become a therapist.

I enrolled in graduate classes at night and, for the next two years, worked toward a master's degree in psychology, the next step toward becoming a psychotherapist. The coursework was invigorating, but I was always falling behind on housework and trying to meet my kids' needs. After earning my degree, I had to complete 3,000 supervised hours providing treatment before I could take the state licensing exam.

I wanted to do for others what Rosalyn had done for me. She had changed my life. I believed therapy could save the world, so I became an evangelist for it.

Once again, I was a true believer. I had found a new kind of magic—a way to make things turn out right.

Transitions

1986–1989

Greg fought for custody of the kids and hired the most expensive shark lawyer in town. He left notes stuck on my car windshield that God hated me. Though I didn't wish him ill, I didn't want to be his wife. He saw it as rebellion and betrayal.

"Look," I told him, "If we cooperate with co-parenting, the kids will do fine. We can share custody. I don't want to push you out of their lives." I tried to explain my vision to him, but he only smoldered. Consumed with anger, he wanted to cut me in the most profound way he could. He would take my children away. Their father, who had never spent time with them and worked on every holiday, wanted to remove me from their lives. And he would use God to do it.

"Your mother has left Jesus and is going to hell," he told the kids while sitting in Burger King. My daughter, who was eight, cried and told me she was embarrassed that he made them all clasp hands in the restaurant while he prayed aloud over their burgers and fries.

My lawyer cost me ten thousand dollars, which I put on a credit card. The divorce took three years because Greg fought to cut me out of the kids' lives completely. I'd never been angrier.

I eventually won sole custody after the court ordered a psychological evaluation to determine the best parenting arrangement. Greg didn't pass due to "psychoticism" and "religiosity."

After a two-year internship in a drug treatment center, I was licensed as a psychotherapist at age 29, and I easily passed my state licensing exams. I bought a used black Miata. I worked with people with addictions, in a battered women's shelter, and at a rape crisis center – all places that felt familiar. I found the work fascinating but never difficult. I understood these people. It all came naturally to me, though it didn't pay much.

I felt old before I turned 30, but I loved to work with teenagers from uncommon backgrounds who had trouble finding their way. I knew rebuilding a life after losses, mistakes, and disasters was possible. I believed anybody could do it over time with intention and a plan. All good things were possible. I told no one about my history with religion, though the decisions I had made at 15 would haunt me for the rest of my life.

PART IV

"This much I know: that eventually, we all have to start screaming well before we hit the ground so the women below us will understand when to scatter, when to take cover, and when it is safe to come back outside and try again to change the world. So that future generations will know, from the echo of our voices, never to stop watching the sky."

Gina Frangello
BLOW YOUR HOUSE DOWN

The Black Leather Jacket

1987

I perched on a metal stool with a red vinyl seat near the front door of Happy Jack's Tavern. Happy Jack's was an old-fashioned bar on a corner of Main Street in my small Central Coast town. A fluorescent sign flickered on and off in the front window, just above a hand-lettered sign reading "Live Music."

The space was a basic long rectangle with a few booths on the perimeter and a smattering of tall tables circled with bar stools. A long, shellacked mahogany bar framed the right side of the room, and the dim yellow glow from sparsely set ceiling lights wasn't strong enough to banish the darkness. The air smelled like stale beer and urine.

No one remembered who Jack was, but the tavern that carried his name catered to serious drinkers. Local garage bands played on weekend nights on a raised platform at the far end of the bar, just in front of the pool tables in the back. Happy Jack's was known as the local commercial fishermen's hangout, a hard-living bunch fond of alcohol and meth. There'd been a stabbing there the year before, two men fighting over a woman. I was there strictly to see Robert. Until I'd met him, I'd never been to a bar.

Robert had a carefully curated bad-boy swagger and a killer black leather jacket. He wasn't classically handsome but had magnetic confidence and attitude. I watched him set up with the other guys in the band and felt a flutter in my chest when he looked up to catch my eye and saunter toward me.

"Hey beautiful," he said, reaching over to pull me off the stool and give me a bear hug and a kiss. He smelled like shampoo and weed and had a soft, magic touch. Robert liked public displays of affection to let the other guys in the band know he now had the advanced status that came with a girlfriend. We'd been dating for two weeks.

Robert was the first guy I dated after Greg. The attachment was intense and instant. Two months after we met, he moved in with me and would become my second husband a year later.

Wild-spirited and mercurial, Robert dropped me into the exciting world of an adolescence I'd never experienced. However, at 27 and a mother of three elementary school kids, I was dramatically off-kilter.

I had no experience dating. All I knew was that I wanted someone very different from Greg; I found that in Robert.

Robert identified as a Jewish atheist, was passionate, dramatically affectionate, and effusive with compliments. He also made me laugh. Above all else, Robert was fun, and he made me feel loved.

The percussionist in the band, he had a lengthy history with cocaine and marijuana. I cared for neither and discouraged both. He was Greg's polar opposite. For the first time in my life, I went to nightclubs, danced, and learned to drink alcohol—though sparingly since more than two drinks made me puke.

"Hey baby, let me get you a drink. Vodka/tonic? If I can borrow your Visa, I can open a tab at the bar. I'll pay you back later after Tommy pays me."

"Sure," I said, without thinking, and pulled my credit card out of my wallet. Robert had lost his cards when he'd filed for bankruptcy the year before I met him. He'd had a stretch of bad luck, but I was confident he was on the path to setting it all right again. He was so brilliant that I was sure he'd make things work out.

Sipping at the drink relieved my jitters. While Robert went back to arrange drums and percussion equipment, I moved closer to the stage so that the scraggly-looking men coming in would realize I was with the band.

Of course, there were red flags everywhere with Robert, but I didn't see them. A wiser person could have checked off boxes: bad debts, lost jobs, conflicts with authority, a pattern of short-term, dramatic relationships that always ended badly, and perhaps most telling, anger problems.

Robert and I met working at a residential treatment center for mentally ill teenagers, where we were both counselors. However, he was soon fired for a profanity-spewing angry outburst at one of the teenage boys who challenged him.

After that, Robert became a self-employed gardener. Though he had a BA in psychology, he was content to mow lawns and perform classic rock covers in dive bars on weekend nights. It gave him lots of free time, and he didn't have to answer to anyone.

On a good night, his cut of the door was fifty bucks.

Robert was the son of a pathologist, and his childhood home had been in Beverly Hills. His older brother was a neurosurgeon, and his sister was a prestigious LA corporate attorney. He'd done his best to rebel against his family; being with me was part of that script. "My mother and sister would hate you if they ever met you – they'd call you a shiksa with kids."

His mother reportedly used Yiddish for pejoratives. Fortunately, his family had cut ties with him years before, so I didn't have to worry about meeting them.

The band was supposed to start at 9:00, but it was 9:35 before the dark-haired leader, Tommy, said into the mic, "Ladies and gentlemen, we are Tommy Lee and the Portagees! We're going to start tonight with some old-time rock'n'roll! Get ready to boogie."

They always opened with *Old Time Rock'n'roll.* Many of Tommy's musical selections made me groan, but I smiled and made eye contact with Robert, who played conga drums. He lit up in front of the audience; his personality dominated whatever room he was in. He oozed superficial charm and could be floridly obsequious when it suited him. He was a master role-player.

People laughed at his clever jokes and impersonations. He could compose himself into any character that suited him. He was also foul-mouthed and often offensive, crossing lines like the most controversial standup comics. Most people laughed and compared him to George Carlin.

When I'd finished my drink, I was ready to dance, so I stood to sway to the reggae-flavored *Red, Red Wine* on the dance floor. When a ponytail-tailed, gray-bearded guy in dirty jeans approached and asked me to dance with him, I smiled and said, "No, thank you. My boyfriend is in the band." I nodded toward Robert. This pattern would repeat throughout the night.

When the band took a break after 30 minutes, Robert would return, down another vodka, and give me more hugs and kisses. "You're the most beautiful woman in the room," he said, whispering in my ear while gazing into my eyes and stroking my hair. The affection and flattery were intoxicating. My mood soared; this was all new. I could barely keep my feet on the ground.

I stopped drinking after two drinks and was sleepy by midnight. I wanted to get some rest but didn't want to leave Robert. I used the payphone outside the door to call home and check in with the high school girl babysitting my kids. Everyone was asleep, and I decided to stay at Happy Jack's until the band broke down at 1:00 am.

I danced alone to David Bowie's *Rebel Rebel,* one of my favorites, and entertained myself by watching the crowd of increasingly drunken dancers flail around the floor. At 1:00 am, I closed out the tab with the bartender.

As the band broke down the equipment, there was a change in vibe. Robert's face was tense as he spoke with Tommy, and I could hear him say, "Yeah, well fuck off, asshole," as he packed his drums into the carry bag. Jumping off the stage, he roughly grabbed my arm and said, "C'mon," as he pulled me out the door.

Somehow, a switch had flipped. His face had contorted, and his eyes had a strange, wild look, which made my chest tighten.

"Fuck that mother fucker," he said through gritted teeth as I allowed him to grab me by the elbow and propel me toward the back of the building to the parking lot.

"What happened?" I said, "What's wrong?"

Turning toward me, he leaned into my face. "Don't fucking ask questions!" he screamed; his pupils were so dilated that his eyes looked black. Instantaneously, I grew smaller and then wholly numb. He shouted, louder this time, "You don't get it, do you? Fuck you too! You don't care! Goddammit, no one ever cares! I can't get a break!"

Striding to his gray Toyota truck, he began kicking his bumper hard and yelling, "Fuck! Fuck! Fuck!"

Shrinking, I was rooted to the spot, heart kicking my sternum. I stood, silently witnessing.

The rage lasted about 10 minutes before he collapsed on the truck with ragged, deep breathing. I tried to soothe him by rubbing his back, as I did with my children when they had tantrums. "Tell me what's wrong," I said, "let's sit in the truck and talk about it."

His tone shifted abruptly as he slumped over the steering wheel, crying desperate sobs. Tommy had refused to pay him the $50 because he'd given him an advance the week before.

"I'm just a loser, I'm broke, I couldn't even cover the bar tab," he said, channeling sorrow.

Rubbing comfort into his back muscles, I assured him he was a stunningly wonderful person. I didn't care about the bar tab. I felt so sorry for him.

After he followed me back to my place, I spent the night holding him. I knew how to calm upset people. I was just what Robert needed. I told myself that we were good for each other. He woke up sweet and cheery the following day and said nothing about the night before. He made pancakes for everyone, and then we took the kids to the beach to fly kites.

It was a wonderful day. He moved in with me a month later.

Togetherness

1987

Living with Robert, I laughed and cried more than I ever had. Life became a perpetual adventure ride down a white-water rapid. I was no longer out of touch with my emotions. Everything felt expansive, exciting, and colorful.

On good days, most days, Robert was warm and effusive. He complimented me, told me I was intelligent and made me feel beautiful. The affection was new, and it felt like a drug. I had never been loved like this, and I soaked it up and craved more.

We filled our days with adventures—hiking, camping, kayaking. Robert loved to cook, and our house often buzzed with guests, laughter, and good food. My friends mostly liked him, though some raised eyebrows at his lawn-mowing job and shaky finances. "It's temporary," I'd assure them. "He's just figuring things out." I said, believing it myself.

Robert was kind to my kids, never trying to be a father figure but always fun and playful with them. They saw him as a buddy, and that was good enough for all of us.

But there was a darker side to Robert. He possessed a native deceptiveness, often exaggerating stories or bending the truth to fit his needs. His casual relationship with facts left me constantly on edge, and his shameless flirting with other women gnawed at my self-esteem. I'd catch him in lies—small ones, that made no sense—and I was often unsettled. When I'd confront him, he'd explode, turning the tables until I felt guilty for even questioning him.

"Maybe you're not cut out for monogamy," I once suggested, trying to make sense of it all. "If it's not for you, maybe we should go our separate ways."

He would always protest, "No, baby, don't say that. You're the love of my life. I don't want anyone but you."

I wanted to believe him. So, I pushed my doubts down and tried to will myself to trust him again.

Then there was the money—or lack thereof. I paid for everything, working long hours in non-profit agencies and my private practice to keep us afloat. Robert contributed $250 a month, calling it "rent." It wasn't enough, but I let it slide, hoping things would improve. Eventually, after months of arguing, he upped it to $600, but that hardly balanced the scales.

I'd occasionally get frustrated and bring it up. "You need to find something that pays more than mowing lawns," I'd say.

That's all it took. His face would flush red with anger, and he'd scream inches from my face. "You don't want me to be happy! You're a controlling bitch!"

I would break down, retreat into tears, and drop the topic, feeling guilty for making him angry. Somehow, I convinced myself that I could work harder, earn more, and make it all work. I was strong. I could handle it.

After all, no man was perfect. Robert had so many good qualities. I clung to those.

One afternoon, I got a voicemail from my friend Brandy. "Shavaun, I saw Robert at the record store this afternoon, smoking weed in the back. He came up to me and specifically told me not to tell you I saw him. I just thought you should know. I don't keep secrets, especially not from friends."

My heart sank. Why would he be sneaky about something like that? Why tell Brandy to keep it a secret? My mind raced, trying to piece it together. He was supposed to be working, not hanging out at a record store. The fact that he'd told Brandy to lie to me was what bothered me most. If he was hiding this, what else was he keeping from me?

The kids were at their dads, so that evening, I confronted him. "So, you saw Brandy today at the record store?" I said as he walked in, covered in grass clippings. "Why would you tell her not to mention it to me?"

He exploded. "Brandy's a crazy fucking bitch! She's trying to stir up trouble. And you—you're controlling! You want to ruin my life! What's wrong with taking a few hours off?"

He grabbed a saltshaker off the table and hurled it across the room, shattering it. I froze, the familiar fear reaction washing over me again. I retreated into the bedroom and closed the door, my heart thumping. I crawled under the covers, trying to calm myself as I listened to him stomp around the house, cursing. Eventually, it grew quiet.

After about an hour, his mood had shifted. He came into the bedroom and, in a calm voice, told me he had made dinner, as if nothing had happened. I got up, pretending everything was fine, and sat down to eat with him.

Robert was manipulative; I could see that. But was I really the "controlling bitch" he claimed I was? His outbursts and gaslighting left me questioning everything. Maybe the problem was me. Maybe I was the one at fault.

For Victims and Survivors

1989–1992

While establishing my private practice and sharing office space with other therapists, I worked part-time for several agencies to supplement my income. Two of those roles left a profound impact: working at the local Women's Shelter Program and the Rape Crisis Center. These non-profits, with missions that resonated with me, gave me the chance to support women and survivors of trauma and abuse in meaningful ways.

The Rape Crisis Center felt like a natural fit. I used to say that gang rape was the number one team sport in my high school. During my four years of high school in the Inland Empire, three of my closest girlfriends had been gang-raped after becoming drunk at parties. None of them reported the attacks, ashamed and afraid, while boys in the hallways snickered when we passed. The silence and stigma surrounding those assaults infuriated me. These boys got away with it.

The Center was a modest stucco building downtown, close to the courthouse and near the university—ideal, since we often accompanied clients to court, and many college women needed our services. Inside, the space was warm and welcoming, with pale yellow walls adorned with cheerful floral prints. Staff brought fresh flowers from their gardens, creating an air of care and healing.

I met with clients twice a week at the Center. To look professional in court, I bought two white button-down shirts, black slacks, and a blazer from Target. My work ranged from supporting survivors as young as four to an elderly woman I'll call Beverly, the oldest survivor I counseled at 89 years old.

Despite her frail appearance—her back hunched from osteoporosis and her hair a halo of white curls—Beverly was a portrait of grace. Sitting across from me on a beige sofa, she spoke calmly, her voice steady despite the tremble in her hands.

"I was watching TV in the afternoon when the doorbell rang," she began, her gaze unwavering. "I looked out the window and saw a clean-cut young man. I thought nothing of it and opened the door. I'm so ashamed now for being so foolish," she said, her voice breaking.

"Beverly," I said gently, "there's no shame here. You had no reason to think anyone would hurt you—you can't blame yourself for being kind."

Victims often blamed themselves, no matter how violent the crime.

"He asked to use my phone," she said. "The moment I hesitated, he pushed the screen door in and knocked me down."

Her assailant, a 30-year-old serial rapist, had fractured her arm, given her black eyes, and left her with a concussion. It was miraculous she wasn't killed. He was later caught, but not before raping four other women. Beverly's courage in testifying against him was awe-inspiring. Her bravery led to his conviction and imprisonment, and I felt immense pride in walking beside her through the trial.

In addition to adults, I counseled many younger survivors, including some boys. Fathers or stepfathers were often the perpetrators, but sometimes, the assailants were groups of men at bars or members of a sports team. I accompanied survivors through court trials and often read their victim impact statements during sentencing. Sadly, the system didn't always bring justice. Many survivors never reported their attacks, too weighed down by shame and self-blame to face the legal system.

Since the Women's Shelter was at a secret location, Marianne, the tall, commanding executive director, interviewed me at a coffee shop downtown for the role of lead therapist. I was excited—the part-time position seemed like a perfect fit. After we discussed my background, she asked one final, crucial question.

"Many women who come to the shelter don't end up leaving their abusers. Why do you think that is?"

I didn't hesitate. "Sometimes they struggle to even recognize they're being abused. They minimize it. Many grew up in families where they became used to mistreatment, and their partners convince them it's all their fault."

"Exactly," she said, smiling. "I like you. When can you start?"

The shelter was in a sprawling, worn-down house with six bedrooms crammed with bunk beds. The house had a moldy smell, but its large, tree-filled lot, rose gardens, and playground offered a peaceful respite from the chaos many women had fled. Most of the residents had experienced severe violence and had no resources. Some struggled with substance abuse or had even abused their own children. It was tough, complex work with no quick fixes.

I led individual and group therapy for the residents and their children. Some of their stories haunted me. At night, I'd wake up from their nightmares invading my sleep. The work taught me that vicarious trauma was real—you could absorb it just by listening.

Celeste was one such woman. In her mid-fifties and rail-thin, her face was a roadmap of pink, jagged scars. Her husband had attacked her with a broken beer bottle while raping her years earlier, and although he'd served time in prison, she had taken him back after his release. By the time I met her, she had come and gone to the shelter nine times.

Celeste's eyes were vacant as she explained that she couldn't stay away from him. It seemed like an addiction. She perceived herself to be trapped, powerless. She'd come to the shelter for a brief time but always returned home. During one session, I tried a different approach. "Celeste let's talk about planning your funeral. You know he'll eventually kill you. By going back, this is how you've chosen to die."

Her eyes widened. For the first time, she didn't know how to respond. "I don't think he'll kill me," she said slowly, "I know he loves me... but maybe... maybe that's how it will end."

Despite our efforts, Celeste returned to him again. I never learned what became of her, though I feared the worst.

Deborah, on the other hand, had a different story. She was well-kept, well-spoken, and intelligent; she was in her early forties when she arrived at the shelter with her two young children. Her husband, a pathologically jealous dentist, had broken every finger in her hand, suspecting her of having an affair.

"I want to leave him, but I'm afraid he'll kill me," she said. "He's threatened to take the kids away, and I can't afford a lawyer. He's taken away all my access to money."

"We'll help you make a plan," I said. Our paralegal helped Deborah file for divorce and get a restraining order. Eventually, she relocated to Arizona, where she had family.

Cases like Deborah's gave me hope. But amid all this, I couldn't ignore the irony: while I helped women escape abusive relationships, I was living with a man who regularly unleashed his anger on me. Yet, compared to Celeste or Deborah, my situation felt far less extreme. There were no bruises, no scars, no broken bones. Robert wasn't jealous or controlling, and he was getting professional help. I clung to that hope, believing that, with time, things would get better.

I still had faith.

Nuclear Power

1980s–90s

Road rage was inevitable when Robert was behind the wheel. One Saturday night, he drove my white Toyota Corolla as we headed 30 miles to a friend's birthday party. We both looked forward to the evening; the mood was light when we left the house. But that didn't last.

The party was on an unfamiliar, unlit country road in the hills. Robert missed a turn, and soon, we were lost, circling desolate, rutted roads in the dark. Before cell phones and GPS, there was no way to call for directions. I could feel his frustration building as he drove faster and more erratically. When we hit a particularly deep rut, my head banged against the window. "Ow!" I said.

"Fuck! Fuck! Fuck!" Robert screamed, slamming his fists into the steering wheel after yet another dead end. He pulled off the road in a rage. I cowered in the passenger seat, taking deep breaths.

"It's okay," I said softly, trying to keep the situation calm. "We'll get there, even if we're a little late."

He whipped his head around, his eyes wild. "You're no help at all! Why can't you do anything? What good are you?" His fist shook dangerously close to my face. I shrank down, staying silent, my heart racing.

He continued to pound the steering wheel, cursing the dark roads and the party in a way that made no sense. Anything I said now would only make it worse and I waited it out.

After ten minutes, Robert's rage subsided. He took a deep breath, set his jaw, and restarted the car. Eventually, we found the narrow dirt road leading to the party.

As soon as we arrived, Robert became his usual charming self, cracking jokes and making everyone laugh within minutes. But I felt numb. I struggled to make conversation, my head still aching. I spent most of the night sitting quietly by myself.

I knew this wasn't normal. But I had convinced myself that this was just Robert's way, that I could handle it. The following week he was back to his kind and nurturing self. Every night he made dinner. He gave me back rubs. He played with the kids. It was so easy to forget Saturday night.

One afternoon, I came home early from work while the kids were at school and found Robert blasting a Jimi Hendrix album. Tiny shards of wood were scattered across the living room floor.

"What happened?" I asked, confused.

Robert's jaw clenched, his face hardening. "Don't fucking talk about it," he growled through gritted teeth. I knew better than to press further. I turned and quickly left to pick up the kids, hoping to avoid another explosion. I took them to Taco Bell for dinner, following up with an outing to the park.

Two hours later, when we returned, the shards of wood were gone, and Robert was back to being calm and pleasant, even serving chocolate ice cream for dessert. I stayed on edge, careful not to say anything that might trigger another episode.

It was two weeks later when I found out what had happened. "Tommy pissed me off, so I smashed my guitar," Robert said casually one evening. I nodded, saying nothing. He had destroyed his own guitar in a fit of rage, a perfect snapshot of his erratic behavior. Years would pass before he bought another one.

One Sunday night, as I was folding laundry, I heard Robert shout, "Goddammit! Fuck!" followed by a loud crash.

Here we go again, I thought, cautiously peeking out of the bedroom to see what had happened. Robert was pacing like a caged animal in front of the TV, which now lay smashed on the floor. He rubbed his fist, grimacing in pain.

"What's wrong?" I asked carefully.

"The goddamn TV is broken!" he yelled. He had punched it in a fit of rage, cracking the screen. I quietly went back to the bedroom and focused on folding the laundry, willing myself to stay calm.

Robert never brought it up again, though he did replace the TV a month later.

Robert's explosive outbursts became regular—once a week or so. My kids and I referred to them as "tantrums." They usually lasted from five to 30 minutes, and I knew to stay out of his way when the storm hit.

The physical intimidation could be overwhelming. Robert would scream inches from my face, his pupils dilated, veins bulging in his temples. Sometimes, he shoved me around the room or threw me onto the bed, but he never actually struck me. Still, I felt trapped. Over time, I began to believe that, somehow, it was all my fault.

He used his rage to scare me into submission. And in the early years, it always worked. Once I was crying or cowering, he'd switch gears, adopting a pathetic, remorseful demeanor. He'd pull me close, apologizing, often with tears, and beg me not to leave. In those moments, I couldn't help but feel sorry for him. The cycle would start again, with a brief honeymoon period filled with affection and tenderness before the next explosion.

My emotional life was a cyclone, but I believed I was strong enough to cope with it. I survived on faith that it was going to get better.

When I tried to have a serious conversation about the anger outbursts, Robert always said, "I've never hit you," to justify his behavior. "I'm only blowing off steam." According to him, it would only be abuse if he used a fist, though he threw me down on the bed on one occasion with his hands around my throat, yelling, "I'm going to squeeze your neck until your brain comes out of your ears!"

But he was strategic, not stupid. He knew never to cross the unforgivable line of directing anger at my kids. He kept the worst of his behavior out of their sight, behind our bedroom door, or on weekends when they visited their dad. Nonetheless, they were aware of some of it.

My ability to compartmentalize was astounding.

Over time, I came to realize that his rage was familiar —like my mother's. But this time, I thought I could change it. I had faith that I could stop the cycle and that things could get better. Even though I wasn't religious anymore, I still believed in miracles.

The Search

1990s

I searched for an explanation for his behavior that would clear him of responsibility. The emphasis in my university studies had been on the developmental damage and lingering effects of childhood trauma and how therapy healed people. Robert had an undergraduate degree in psychology, so he was well-versed in the theories.

He was adept at acting out trauma stories from his childhood as a colorful form of entertaining improv at parties. He'd been performing his schtick in front of friends for years. Acting came naturally to him.

Robert impersonated his parents and siblings to illustrate how hard he'd had it as a kid. He mimed an upper-class, caustic, attention-seeking mother who got sloppy drunk and spewed curses in Yiddish. His angry father had committed suicide when he was seven years old.

"Yeah, my old man offed himself," he'd say glibly over a pasta meal with guests. The dramatic stories always captured people's attention and gained him sympathy. However, the reported family trauma history didn't adequately explain the type and intensity of his rage episodes.

His behavior didn't fit the typical symptoms of PTSD. I decided he must have ADHD or bipolar disorder and thus be biologically unable to regulate his moods. There had to be a problem with his brain chemistry, and I started studying medications that might help.

Through my benevolent lens, I saw Robert as a traumatized victim who would eventually recover with love, support, and therapy. And there was lots of therapy. I paid one therapist after another.

He enjoyed therapy—he loved to talk about himself. Sometimes, I sat in, or we tried marriage counseling, but I was careful never to disclose anything in front of Robert that could cause him to blow up at me later.

I could never speak privately with anyone treating him individually since the therapeutic relationship was sacrosanct. There was no way to say it if I couldn't say it in front of Robert; clearly, I couldn't. Though he could entertain all the mental health clinicians with his humor and charm, the rage episodes never abated.

Of course, I realize now that was because he never told any of them about his anger, dark moods, or aggression; thus, they had no way of knowing. If they didn't know, it couldn't be addressed. Above all, Robert was a showman who knew how to give people exactly what he wanted them to see.

Faith and Hope

1994

I leased a sunny, two-office suite on the upper floor of an older Spanish-style house next to the city park for my private practice. It was a peaceful, charming space, with a fireplace and windows that framed the towering pine trees outside. I filled it with oriental rugs and a blue velvet couch and hung Georgia O'Keeffe prints on the walls. I wanted my clients to step into comfort, to feel safe and welcome in this haven I had created.

Even though I was no longer working directly for the Women's Shelter or Rape Crisis Center, they continued to send me referrals. Trauma recovery had become one of my specialties, and I felt deeply connected to the survivors I worked with. I knew all too well how violence, coercive control, and verbal abuse could shape a person's life. I had helped dozens of people leave toxic relationships. And yet, despite my expertise, I couldn't seem to protect myself from the very thing I was so skilled at recognizing in others.

Soothing Robert became part of the natural rhythm of my life. I was the personal fire extinguisher for his combustible moods. As a healer, I took my work seriously both inside and outside the office. I immersed myself in continuing education workshops, studied the latest research, and built a library full of books promising new approaches to treating troubled people. If there was a solution, I was determined to find it.

My willingness to work with the most challenging clients earned me a strong reputation, one that brought constant referrals. I took it as a compliment at the time, though now I see it differently. Perhaps I was simply accepting clients others refused to work with. I supervised interns, built a thriving practice, and gained the trust of my peers. Many of my clients were clinicians themselves. I felt confident in my career, even as my personal life continued to be tumultuous.

I told no one about Robert's tantrums, not even the therapist I saw periodically. To admit the truth out loud would have forced me to confront the reality that I needed to leave. Bad things have a way of solidifying when spoken, and I wasn't ready to face that. I wasn't talking, and so the reality of my life remained unspoken, suspended in silence.

I call this now a *negative hallucination*—the inability to see what's right in front of you.

Deeper down, I had never fully shed the message that I was a sinner, still carrying around the shame I had acquired in childhood. I had no skills in setting personal boundaries. The threat of Robert's rage was familiar, like an old coat that still fit. I could tolerate so much—far more than I should have. And for years, I never once called it abuse.

After all, Robert never hit me.

Whenever I was close to leaving, Robert's pitiful side would emerge like clockwork. He sensed when I was at my breaking point and would lay his failures bare—his inability to land a good job, his endless self-loathing. "I'm a loser," he'd say through tears. "A fuck-up. A fool." He was masterful at invoking sympathy, especially when it came to his own tears. There was something about a man crying that melted me every time.

I would soothe him, offer encouragement, and in return, he'd promise to "get it together." He vowed to stop the volatile behavior, and I believed him. I'd push him back into therapy, suggest antidepressants, and throw myself into studying the latest treatments. He tried hypnotherapy and EMDR, cycled through antidepressants and ADHD medication.

None of it made a difference.

But I kept holding on. I believed that the real Robert was the one who loved me and nurtured me. The angry Robert was just a symptom that could be fixed with enough love and care. So, I held onto faith and clung to hope.

I waited for the day when Robert would be healed.

A Resume

1994

I arrived home from the office at 5:30 p.m., hit play on the blinking answering machine, and heard an unfamiliar, upbeat female voice. "Hi, this is Monique. I'm calling for Robert. I hope it's okay if I call. Tommy gave me the number. Are you still up for happy hour tomorrow night to help me with my resume? Call me back."

My heart began to pound. Happy hour? Resume? I thought he had band practice on Tuesday nights. And, of course, her name was Monique—a name that conjured images of someone chic and glamorous. Knowing Robert, she had to be attractive. He wasn't one to cozy up to women unless he found them visually appealing, despite his oft-repeated claims of being "just a nice, friendly guy."

Without thinking, I acted on impulse. I punched in the number she'd left, and Monique answered on the first ring. Keeping my voice calm and professional, I told her I was Robert's wife returning her call and I could pass along a message to him. Where was he supposed to meet her for happy hour?

"Oh!" she gasped, clearly caught off guard. "I didn't know he was married. I'm so sorry; tell him I'll handle it myself. Thank you for letting me know." She hung up abruptly, without saying goodbye.

I fumed, my heart pumping. I knew I couldn't keep quiet, but confronting Robert meant facing a predictable volcanic eruption. I sat in the bedroom, pondering and waiting.

"So, who is Monique?" I asked as he walked in an hour later, his clothes speckled with dried mud. My voice was tight, my body braced for the inevitable.

His brow furrowed, and he exploded. "What the fuck, you don't trust me now?" he yelled. "You don't have the right to question me—you don't know anything about what I do. I'm just being helpful—I'm a nice guy, How fucking dare you!"

"I returned her call," I said, keeping my voice calm. "She was very nice, but she had no idea you were married."

In an instant, he was on me. As he shoved me hard with both hands, I fell backward, my head hitting the floor. Grabbing my jeans by the waistband, he began jerking me around like a ragdoll while he yelled in my face.

When I started to cry, he dropped me, only to whirl around and punch the drywall. His hand swelled almost immediately.

"You need to shut up about things!" he yelled, shaking his injured hand. "You always provoke me! You're the reason I have to let off steam!" He stormed off to the bathroom, slamming the door behind him.

Still crying, I grabbed my purse and keys, slipped out the front door, and drove back to my office. There, I curled up on the couch under a throw, too shaken to do anything else. Two hours later, he called, and I let the phone go to voice mail. He kept calling. After the third time, I picked up.

"Hey babe, I'm sorry. I shouldn't have lost it like that. I made stir fry for dinner. Please come home. I miss you."

I felt my resolve crumble, as it usually did. Maybe I was being jealous. Maybe I was neurotic. Was this all my fault? Should I have kept quiet? I couldn't trust my instincts—self-doubt had become second nature. I had no one to confide in and nowhere else to go. I had to work in the morning, I needed to go home.

When I returned, Robert was affectionate, as if nothing had happened. Later that night, he wanted to make love and tried to hold me tight, but I couldn't shut off my mind. I lay there, feeling frozen, knowing deep down that whatever this was, it wasn't right.

His hand stayed swollen and purple for weeks, but we never spoke of it again. The hole in the bedroom wall remained for years.

The Color of Collars

1995

In my mid-30s, I already had three teenagers—one about to graduate from high school. Many of my peers were just starting their families, while I was busy worrying about how to help mine navigate college. Finances were tight, and while I wanted to support whatever path my kids chose, I never pressured them about college.

"It's your life and your decision," I would tell them.

"Whatever you choose, make sure it's for you, not for me. You have to find your own path."

We agreed they'd begin at community college, just as I had. It was a more affordable option, and since they'd be working part-time, they could go at their own pace. Pell grants, student loans, and maybe even scholarships would help bridge the gap.

Living in a small town, I often crossed paths with
academics from the local university, whether I wanted to
or not. A former co-worker, now married to a retired
English professor, invited me to a networking dinner at
their home—an elegant affair with cocktail shrimp,
caviar, and canapés. The house, perched on a hill with
sweeping views of the city, was immaculately designed,
more like a showroom than a home. Most of the guests
were older, retired professors, effortlessly discussing
European vacations and the ins and outs of getting their
children into upper-tier law and medical schools.

I knew how to dress for the occasion. I wore a green
silk dress from Banana Republic, which cost more than
I should've spent, but it helped me play the part. Over
the years, I'd honed my ability to blend in, to look like I
belonged even when I felt utterly out of place.

As the dinner conversation dragged on, my dis-com-
fort grew. The academic one-upmanship about prestigious schools and family legacies bored me. After the
meal, I retreated to a corner of the living room, flipping
through a glossy *Condé Nast* magazine, silently counting
the minutes until I could make a graceful exit.

An older couple sat down across from me, their
conversation catching my ear. He, in a suit and tie,
leaned toward his wife, who wore a sleek black cocktail
dress.

"You know, these scholarship programs don't really
do much," he said, his voice dripping with con-descen-
sion. "These blue-collar families work so hard to get
their kids into college. They're so proud when it happens. But the truth is, blue-collar can't go white-collar
for more than one generation. The next generation

always goes back to being plumbers or auto mechanics. It's inevitable."

He chuckled, and something inside me cracked.

"Really?" I said, looking up, inserting myself into their conversation. "I've never heard that before."

"Oh, yes," he replied smugly, clearly not expecting any pushback. "I've seen it many times." He turned to me. "Are you a psychotherapist like Charles?" he asked, referring to the party's co-host.

"Yes, we worked together about ten years ago at a drug treatment center."

His eyes widened. "Oh my! That must have been dreadful work. I can't imagine anyone wanting to do that."

I smiled thinly. "Actually, I found it pleasant. People with addictions usually know they've messed up by the time they get to treatment. They admit they have problems, which gives me something to work with. I much prefer working with them compared to rich people who think they're better than everyone else." I paused, savoring the shift in the room. "Rich people are just as messed up—they just refuse to admit it. You can't help someone who doesn't think they need it."

His smile froze on his face, and the air between us turned icy. His wife, sensing the tension, stepped in to save the conversation.

"Well, it was lovely meeting you, dear," she said with forced cheer. "Are you married? What does your husband do?"

"Yes," I nodded. "I'm married. My husband is a gardener."

"Oh, a landscape architect?" she asked, her eyes brightening at the prospect.

"No," I replied with a small, satisfied smile. "He mows lawns."

I reached into my bag and pulled out one of Robert's business cards for Budget Gardening. "If you ever need your lawn mowed, feel free to call. He can prune your shrubbery, too."

I handed her the card and stood up to leave, grinning as I said goodnight.

Valentine

February 14, 1994

I drive you nuts, I'm stuck in ruts
Will you be my Valentine?
I mess things up like a careless pup.
Will you be my Valentine?
I wake you nights.
To calm my frights
Will you be my Valentine?
I swear I'll change,
I'll rearrange!
Will you be my Valentine?
I'll entertain
To ease your pain
Will you be my Valentine?
I'll be with you all the time.
Yes, I will be YOUR Valentine FOREVER

Love you,

Robert

The Sacred Banyan Tree

1995

Every color is more intense in Hawaii. The blues, greens, and reds are more vivid, giving the world a magical sheen. The scent of tropical blooms hangs heavy in the humid air, mixing with the earthy aroma of rich, damp soil. I'd always wanted to visit Paradise, so I saved up for a week on Maui with Robert. This was the first time I'd left the mainland, and as we drove away from the airport in a rental car, I swore I would never leave. The landscape out the car window left me breathless in a good way.

I had found an isolated vacation rental online, a tiny cottage perched near a cliff with a glass wall facing the ocean. It was on a flower farm owned by a hippie guy named Phil, who also hosted New Age seminars at a larger building on the other side of the acreage. The only sound we could hear was the crashing of the ocean waves. It was so peaceful that I slept for the first 24 hours we were there. Our host brought exotic fruits and pastries every morning, and my nervous system was calmer than it had ever been before. If there was a heaven, this was it.

On the second morning, Phil dropped off breakfast and said, "I must give you a tour and explain the sacred tree. I want you to have all the blessings we offer here."

"Sure," I said, intrigued and only partly tongue-in-cheek. "I'm up for all the blessings I can get."

Robert and I followed Phil around the grounds as he explained the various kinds of fruit trees and flowering plants. "This is Hawaiian ginger," he said, "and these trees over here grow star fruit." There were orchids, passionflower vines, and banana trees. It was all more than I could absorb. "But this is what I really want you to see," he said, leading us to a huge tree that looked 40 feet tall with an enormous girth. "This is our sacred banyan."

"This tree has the power to grant wishes. If you stand beneath it at sunset and meditate to the right vibration, you can visualize your greatest desire, and it will manifest. I'm not kidding. It's part of the Law of Attraction. I explain this to all our guests, and there have been miracles," he said, gesturing expansively with his hands. I listened closely, intrigued.

"The thing is, you can't tell anyone what you wished for. If you do, that breaks the spell. Keep it to yourself, but continue meditating on the outcome you want. If you do that diligently, it will happen."

That evening at sunset, Robert and I stood side by side under the banyan tree, facing the western horizon. I wore a knee-length floral sundress and flip-flops, and my hair was big and puffy from the humidity. Robert wore baggy shorts and a ragged t-shirt, and his sunscreen smelled like coconut oil. The sun was a big orange ball, and the sky was streaked with cobalt, purple, and golden hues. If any place looked like potential miracle territory, this was it.

Squeezing Robert's right hand in mine, I lifted my other palm to the sky in supplication, just as I had in Pastor Raeburn's church twenty years before. I repeated the words silently, "Oh please, sacred tree—let him get a real job." He squeezed my hand back as we looked at each other and smiled. Per instructions, he never revealed what he had wished for.

After Hawaii, I repeated my wish whenever I saw a shooting star. Certainly, an extra wish here and there couldn't hurt.

If we're going to credit sacred trees and planetary bodies for good outcomes, I can say that it took a long time for the miracle to manifest. Four years later, after I again pushed for separation unless he got a steady job, Robert was hired for an entry-level position at the local sewage treatment plant. He increased his financial contribution to the household to $1,200 a month, and, best of all, the job came with health insurance. I was thrilled.

Truck Stop Diners

1995

The truck stop diner smelled like chicken fried steak and despair. I sat in a sticky vinyl booth across from my father, who was at home there. In my childhood fantasies, my father had reminded me of a red-haired JFK—wise, handsome, and strong. He'd never once hit me, never raised his voice. He was the good guy in my story.

But now the hair on his head had grown white, and the skin on his hands thin. I was suddenly more aware of his bones than his muscles. He was seventy and would die of pneumonia later that year.

By then, we lived hundreds of miles apart, and my kids were nearly grown. I saw him no more than twice a year, but when I did, there would always be at least one meal in a truck stop diner—copious plain food and his ability to pay for it easily made them among his favorite places.

"In the orphanage, they wouldn't let you eat until after you said grace," my father said with a smirk, his southern drawl emphasizing the word grace and stretching it out to three syllables.

"I'd sooner starve than say a prayer thanking God for my food, so they made me sit there for hours in silence, and I got nothing to eat. I was used to hunger, but the other kids felt sorry for me, and they'd sneak me an apple or an extra piece of bread. It held me over until I could run away from there with my little brothers."

My dad was born hungry child number 12 in a family of 14 hungry children, just in time for the great depression to hit rural Kansas hard. When his father died when he was seven, my grandmother was forced to deposit her youngest three children in a Nazarene orphanage where she hoped they'd be fed. Many things about religion set my father's teeth on edge, and his experiences in that orphanage were chief among them.

"I got my little brothers, and we snuck out the window when everyone else was sleeping. We ran all night as far as we could get and looked for farms where we could work for room and board. We got by that way until we were old enough to sign up for the military, just in time for World War II."

I was my father's only child, and he was seldom home. Terrified by the perpetual threat of the poverty he'd lived in as a child, he worked long hours every day, including weekends. Dad left childrearing to my mother and didn't complain about my religious indoctrination despite his bitter feelings about faith. He ignored it, as he did most other things about his family.

Though he rarely spoke, when he did, Dad made sure

to have conversations with me about what he thought was most important in life. Most of these conversations revolved around financial matters or, in practical terms, how to keep from starving. He also explained the mechanisms of our government, the importance of unions, and how Roosevelt had saved the country with The New Deal.

I loved his stories. I knew they were important. Before long, the stories would be all I'd have left of him. One of his favorite topics was the folly of credit card debt and how foolish people could easily lose their homes because of buying things they couldn't afford and didn't need. More than anything, he wanted me to understand how interest worked.

My father bought everything in cash, including his car. He'd save for years and purchase only what he could pay for upfront. "Interest is something you earn, never something you pay," he'd say. That adage seared into my brain, along with his work ethic. Relaxing has never come naturally to me.

Driven by fear, my father was known to be miserly. Many found his stinginess cruel. Even when his brothers or stepsons came to him to borrow money, he charged exorbitant amounts of interest and held them to a repayment plan.

As was common in his time, he was not-so-casually misogynistic. Dad found women innately inferior creatures. His most common terms for women were "stupid bitch," "dumb broad," or "old heifer." Occasionally, he'd mention a "pretty sharp gal," but that was the exception to his norm. It didn't strike me as odd when I was a kid, though it shocks me now. This was the water I swam in.

Life with my father was hard on my mother. There was no household division of labor—the labor was all hers. She worked full-time, did the shopping, cooked, cleaned, and hung the laundry out back on the clothesline. Every Saturday, she mowed the lawns and washed the cars while I vacuumed, dusted, and mopped the kitchen. Dad fixed mechanical problems with the cars or big things around the house, like patching the roof when it leaked. But overall, my mother was expected to earn half the income and still take care of everything else.

Though she never protested directly, she seethed. Years after her death, I came to understand more clearly the reasons she filled the house with anger. Before her illness, she confided that she'd stood up to him on one occasion several years before my birth, and he'd punched her in the jaw, knocking her to the ground. He never hit her again, but she knew better than to challenge him directly.

I had a hard time imagining it; the man who punched my mother was not the father I thought I knew. I've had to look at him through a prism to see that the hero in my story could be the villain in someone else's.

My father seldom looked my way, but when he did, he smiled. He rarely spoke to me, but when he did, he was kind.

The deprivation of his childhood had left Dad an emotional amputee; though uneducated, he was not a stupid man, and he could have been a hero if not for the parts of him that had been severed, leaving him with an insatiable hunger that consumed our family from within.

He was obsessive, single-minded, and driven. He left

me hungry for male attention when I was growing up. Nevertheless, my father gave me everything he had to give. Sometimes, the world is a chicken-fried steak and a lesson about interest. The greatest sacrifice you may know how to make is keeping your family fed.

The Cash Advance

1997

It was a sweltering summer day, and I left the office early on a Friday. I stopped at the end of our dirt road to grab the mail from the postal box, a familiar cloud of dust enveloping my Toyota. The mail was delivered late in the afternoon; typically, Robert made sure to get there before I did to collect it. I never questioned this.

A statement from a credit card company I didn't recognize was mixed in with the stack of junk mail. It was addressed to me. Opening it, I was shocked to see that this was a new card with a balance of $10,000 that had been taken as a cash advance in my name. I had never signed up for the card and knew nothing about it. Once again, I felt crazy. I considered calling the police. Who could have done this? I had a sick feeling in my gut.

I was waiting at the dining table when Robert walked in an hour later. "Can you explain this to me?" I asked, holding it up.

Robert blanched, and his eyes widened, but he responded without skipping a beat, "Oh, it's not a problem. I'm helping Johnny out, but he'll pay me back before it's due so I can pay it all off. He got into some legal hot water, but it's not his fault. He's getting it all straightened out."

Johnny was a sketchy friend from the band who sold meth and heroin on the side. I hated him and had made it clear he wasn't welcome at the house around my kids. Incensed, I raised my voice.

"So, you can't help with expenses here, but you're willing to wreck my credit to help Johnny? This is unforgivable! You need to get this money back immediately, or I'll call the cops on both of you."

This time, he didn't flip to rage. Worried I might file a police report, he picked up the phone, "Okay, okay, I'll take care of it." With a theatrical flourish, he punched in Johnny's number, putting it on speaker. He gave the performance of a lifetime. The crying began as soon as Johnny answered. He told him I'd found the credit card statement, and he needed the money back.

"Please, Johnny, please!" he cried, begging, tears streaming down his face and sobs breaking his voice. "Shavaun will kick me out if you don't return the ten grand. I don't have anywhere to go. She's threatening to call the cops."

There was a long pause while Johnny argued. He told Robert that he needed more time. He'd be collecting on some bad debts in a month and could return it then. I stood there grimly and shook my head no.

Robert continued sobbing and pleading. I watched and listened, aghast. The tears seemed so genuine. After ten minutes, Johnny agreed to get him the money by the end of the next week. He hung up the phone and flashed a Cheshire Cat grin. "See babe? I took care of it. It's all fine."

I felt as if someone poured ice water down my back. The masterful performance terrified me. The impact of watching him turn on tears at will hit me harder than any of his other behaviors. I couldn't deny that I was witnessing an entirely conscious manipulation, but I didn't know where to file that knowledge.

Later that night, after Robert had made dinner, he rubbed my shoulders and repeated how much he loved me. "You're the best, babe," he said, kissing the top of my head. "You're my world. You're the smartest person I know."

My thoughts swirled. It felt surreal. Who *was* Robert? I no longer had any inclination to melt into his arms, and I could see that so much was off. Everything about him smelled fishy.

Going forward, I made it a point to get to the mailbox before he did each day. I knew I needed to get out of the relationship, but I couldn't see how to do it.

We started couples counseling again.

Talking Drums

1999

On a breezy Sunday afternoon, I strolled downtown alone when I first heard the thunder of the djembes emanating from the whitewashed building housing the yoga studio. Boom-tah-kah, boom-tah-kah, dum-dum-dum. The rhythms pulsed and echoed through the open windows, drawing me across the street like a magnet.

At nearly 40, I was lean and strong from my active outdoorsy life, but the weight of my daily stress bore down on me. Migraines had become frequent companions, a nagging reminder of the pressure in my head. Though I'd taken yoga classes at the studio before, they offered little solace from my stress or headaches. I glanced at the sign on the door of the charming old building and noticed a newly listed African Dance Class starting at 2:00. I was just a few minutes late.

Following the drums, I climbed the wooden stairs to the second-floor studio. Boom-tah-kah, boom-tah-kah, dum-dum-dum. Peeking through the door, I felt the rhythms vibrating through the floorboards, pulsing around me with a tangible pleasant energy. Inside, a crowd of primarily young women swayed and leaped in unison, creating a powerful connection with a trio of male drummers at the front. I had never witnessed anything quite like it. I stood transfixed until the leader —a tall, striking woman from Africa with long black braids and a dazzling smile—invited me to join the line. "Just follow what I show you," she said, her manner warm and enthusiastic.

With 25 others in the room, we formed lines, moving from front to back in sections, each person mirroring the teacher's graceful movements. The drums didn't merely accompany the dance; they drove it, conversing with the dancers in a dynamic call-and-response. I felt the rhythm seep into my bones.

Though I'd always loved dancing, my inhibitions often held me back. But in that first class, something shifted. My hips swayed, my chest lifted, and my feet pounded the ground, hands thrusting skyward. For the first time, I truly sensed my body—muscles, joints, and bones—and discovered a deep reservoir of physical power. This dance was meant for me.

As the class cooled down, the teacher approached, her smile radiant. "You did great! Feel free to sign up and come back." It felt like a gift, and without a second thought, I registered. The classes quickly became the highlight of my week.

Each session was more than just a dance lesson; it was an endurance exercise that pushed my body to its limits and revealed strength I didn't know I had. I felt like a lioness, fierce and unburdened, as the weight of shame I carried melted away.

We carry trauma in our bodies as much as in our minds. Neural pathways weave through our muscles, tendons, and ligaments, constricting us in patterns of fear and pain. But sometimes, when we shake the body up—when we dance—we shift our perceptions and change our behaviors. We find fresh breath, a new voice, and an undeniable power. We start to see things differently.

Mobile Crisis

2000–2004

My headlights struggled to penetrate the wall of rain before me. The sky was a pitch-black canvas, heavy clouds obscuring any glimpse of the moon or stars. I hunched forward over the steering wheel, my eyes straining to see the yellow lines on the slick road. The windshield wipers worked furiously, sweeping back and forth in a frantic, rhythmic motion, barely keeping pace with the deluge. One of the wipers squeaked incessantly, driving me crazy, but there was nothing I could do about it. The steady roar of water splashing against the van's tires almost drowned out the noise.

I kept my speed below 30 mph because it was 1:30 a.m. on a Saturday, and I had a passenger in the back. The road was mostly deserted, slick, and treacherous. I was working and feeling keyed up, adrenaline coursing through me.

I never imagined I'd be driving a massive, institutional gray van equipped with a metal mesh barrier between the front seat and the back, with a person who wanted to kill me sitting behind me. But there I was, navigating a mountain highway in the middle of the night in the midst of a rainstorm.

The woman in the back believed she was under threat from vampires and wanted to impale me because of it, but thankfully the barrier kept her from reaching me. As long as I kept the van on the road, I trusted I'd be okay.

I was always looking for ways to earn a bit more income with side gigs. A friend told me about Mobile Crisis, a subset of the County Mental Health System that provides emergency mental health treatment out in the community. This meant a solo mental health clinician carried a pager and responded on-site to assess and intervene with individuals facing serious mental health crises. Often, mobile crisis therapists worked alongside law enforcement and other first responders and emergency medical providers.

I applied and was hired immediately over the phone for two 12-hour overnight shifts a week. It wasn't a job that most therapists wanted to sign up for. The pressure and adrenaline were worlds apart from sitting comfortably in an office discussing personal growth for an hour.

In the field, I dealt with psychotic, potentially dangerous people. I had to think fast and act boldly, conducting rapid assessments to determine the most likely diagnoses and coming up with the safest plan on the spot. Each call was a race against time, with another call waiting around the corner.

"Julia, how are you doing back there?" I yelled over my shoulder, straining to make myself heard. The only reply was a hard kick to the back of my seat, jolting me. In the rearview mirror, I caught a glimpse of her sitting upright, staring straight ahead. At least she wasn't trying to escape, but I had to keep an eye on her while navigating the storm. I'd been warned that clients sometimes tried to strangle themselves with seatbelt straps. Fortunately, I had control of the door-locking system; she couldn't make a break for it while I was driving.

Glancing back at her while keeping my eyes on the road was stressful. My shoulders crept up toward my ears, and I felt the familiar ache of an impending migraine throbbing at my temples.

I was transporting Julia to the emergency room next to the inpatient psych unit, a better option for her than jail. I had been called out by a police officer who paged me at midnight, explaining that Julia had been reported for harassing her neighbors in her mobile home park.

"She's been threatening people and calling them vampires," he said, his voice concerned. "She's scared the whole neighborhood. We've tried to calm her down, but she's out of her mind."

This sounded interesting. While it wasn't uncommon for psychotic people to have delusions about evil forces, they usually imagined demons or Satan lurking. I'd never had a case involving vampires before, but I recalled all the popular horror movies on the subject.

Psychotic people could be suggestible. "I'll get there as soon as possible," I assured the officer. "I'm about 45 minutes away."

Of course, the mobile home park was 30 miles out of town and up the grade—the closest thing we had to a coastal mountain. The pouring rain would only slow me down further.

When I finally arrived at the mobile home park, the place was well-kept, and the homes lined up neatly. A police car was parked right in front, and I pulled the van in behind it. As I climbed the four wooden stairs to the front door, moths circled the glowing yellow porch light. I could hear a woman shouting from inside, so I tapped lightly on the door.

A young Latino officer with a furrowed brow opened it. He beckoned me in, whispering, "We've been getting 911 calls about this lady harassing her neighbors for the last 24 hours. She's off her rocker and out of control. I don't know what's wrong with her, but jail isn't the right place for her."

"Sure," I replied. "Let me evaluate her, and I'll see what I can do." He showed me Julia's ID, which indicated she was 69 years old.

Stepping into the small living room, I immediately spotted the source of the yelling. A small, gray-haired woman who looked her age sat on a kitchen chair with an older cop looming over her.

"Let me out of here!" she screamed. "You're all trying to kill me!" I noticed her hands were cuffed behind her back as she thrashed around. She looked like anyone's stereotypical grandmother, with neatly coiffed hair and a floral print top, paired with stretch polyester slacks. A row of blooming African violets lined the windowsill, offering a stark contrast to the chaos. Unlike many homes I entered, this one was neat and clean.

When Julia turned toward me, her eyes widened in fear. "Get out of here! Don't look at me! I know who you are—you're trying to hypnotize me with your eyes! Don't look at me! Don't look at me, you VAMPIRE!"

I wondered how so much volume could come from such a small woman. She sucked all the air out of the room. I was used to crisis clients who weren't happy to see me, but I had never been received quite like this before. Julia made me think of *The Exorcist*.

I raised my palms to cover my face. Blessedly, her shrieks subsided. "It's okay, Julia. My name is Shavaun. I'm here to help you. I'll keep my eyes covered if that makes you feel better. I won't do anything to hurt you, but I need to ask you a few questions."

She responded with a low, guttural growl. I heard the cop next to me sigh—cops dreaded dealing with cases like this.

I stood six feet in front of Julia, giving her plenty of space. With my palms shielding my eyes, I tried to engage her in conversation. "You have a beautiful home, but I understand that you're not feeling safe. I'm sorry about that. Do you have any pets, Julia? A dog or a cat?"

Another growl was her only reply. If she had a pet, someone would need to care for it while I took her to the inpatient unit. I was thinking ahead but saw no signs of animals in the house.

Julia was difficult to assess, though I welcomed the challenge; it was hard because she refused to provide any background or health information. I wondered whether she had any relatives nearby. It was clear she was delusional, indicating a problem with her brain. The symptoms could stem from various conditions—schizophrenia, bipolar mania, or, less likely, a brain injury, dementia, or a drug reaction. Meth was notorious for causing such symptoms, but she didn't fit the profile of a tweaker.

No matter the cause, I decided Julia needed to be hospitalized. She posed a potential risk to herself or others, and jail wasn't the right place for her. The cops were right about that.

The younger officer emerged from the hallway, waving a handful of prescription bottles. I stepped over to inspect them and noted a thyroid supplement, a cholesterol medication, an antidepressant, and an antipsychotic. The presence of the antipsychotic was a red flag, indicating a likely major mental illness. She may have experienced this psychotic episode due to stopping her medication. I meticulously recorded the medications and the names of the prescribing doctors, planning to take them in a bag to the hospital with her.

Turning to the younger cop, I whispered, "I can take her down to County Mental Health Inpatient if you can get her in my van. I have a feeling she could hurt me if I tried to handle her myself."

"Oh, definitely," the cop replied, nodding. "There's a reason we had to cuff her. She'll try to fight. She's been threatening to stake the vampires."

The drive down the mountain felt like the longest vehicle ride of my life. Occasionally, another car passed in the opposite direction, its headlights slicing through the dark momentarily before vanishing. The rain showed no signs of letting up, creating a surreal atmosphere of isolation. This was not a time anyone wanted to have to pull over.

When I arrived at the hospital, two athletic male psych techs escorted Julia out of the van, one on each side. She growled at me again as they led her past. Other than the paperwork to admit her, my job was done. I was relieved she hadn't vomited in the back, which sometimes happened in these situations.

I left the hospital and returned to my van, letting out a breath I didn't realize I had been holding. The drive home felt lighter.

As I pulled onto my street and turned off the headlights, I took a moment to appreciate the relative calmness of my neighborhood. It was 3:30 a.m., and the rain continued to fall gently, creating a soothing rhythm that lulled my senses.

I was on to the next call 20 minutes later. By the time I finished, it was 6:00 a.m., and the sun was climbing above the horizon like a big orange ball. My head felt like it was trapped in a vise, and I was exhausted.

I wasn't easily rattled because I had grown up with strange behavior—the kind induced by tricks of the brain. People hearing voices, believing weird things, and volatile outbursts were all familiar to me. Confident in my abilities most of the time, I felt good about the crisis work. It seemed like I had a natural instinct for de-escalating tense situations.

When things didn't go smoothly, I worked closely with the cops to devise a safe plan where no one got hurt. This meant conducting rapid, thorough assessments to determine the nature and severity of the crisis. Then, a risk assessment followed to identify any immediate danger to the individual or others, especially the potential for self-harm.

I provided emotional support, searched for every available resource, and then worked to come up with the best solution using what was at hand. This often meant arranging for admission to the county psychiatric hospital if there were no other alternatives.

My time with Mobile Crisis had toughened me up. I had to pay close attention to boundaries because, usually, lives really were at stake.

A turning point came after a bad outcome. My colleague, Jeff, had gone to a middle-class family's home, where a 16-year-old had threatened suicide during a fight with his father. The dad had called Mental Health Crisis for help. When Jeff arrived, the teenager swore he hadn't been serious about hurting himself. Though father and son had been fighting, things seemed calm when Jeff assessed the situation.

After counseling both of them, Jeff determined that the threat had been idle. The father agreed not to leave his son alone, and they denied having any firearms in the house. Jeff referred them for therapy, and they planned to make an appointment with a therapist as soon as possible. It looked like a good resolution, so Jeff moved on to the next call.

He had done everything right. We were trained to avoid unnecessary hospitalizations, and none of us would have handled it any differently. But an hour after Jeff left, the teenager shot himself with a gun he and his father had denied having. The boy died instantly in his bedroom.

The next day, all crisis workers were called in for a staff meeting. Incidents like this meant a lawsuit against the agency, and sometimes, personal lawsuits against the clinician. It was my worst nightmare.

Jeff, a young father with two toddlers, sat hunched in a circle of chairs. His shoulders slumped; his face shadowed with grief. He held his head in his hands and groaned.

"I blew it," he said, his mouth contorted. "I should have taken him to the hospital. This is all on me."

"Of course, it's not on you," I said, my voice gentle. "You did what any of us would have done. We're not mind readers. They lied to you about having a gun. You can't control whether people are telling you the truth."

He stared at his lap, shaking his head back and forth, sobbing quietly. The rest of us sat in grim silence, exchanging looks of shared pain. We all felt it.

That was the moment I realized this could just as easily have been me. If it ever happened, I knew I wouldn't be able to handle the guilt. I couldn't bear the thought of making the wrong call and having someone die because of it. I expected too much of myself. I demanded perfection in a job where so much was unpredictable, and the outcomes were often beyond our control.

"Robert, I'm quitting crisis," I said when I got home that night. "I couldn't stand it if someone killed themselves on my watch."

He nodded, his expression understanding. "Yeah, I get it, baby. That's probably for the best. You'd never get over it. You're too sensitive."

Robert knew me, inside and out.

Reality Bites

2000

I was in the kitchen one evening when Robert got home from work. The jerk of his head and the way he slammed his keys down on the counter told me everything I needed to know—he was in one of his dark moods. I stayed calm, locking eyes with him as the words poured out of me.

"I don't know what you're upset about, but if you get in my face again, I'll call 911. You *will* be arrested, and I'll let you sit in jail. You are not getting away with abuse anymore. I'll get a restraining order, and you'll have to leave."

He froze two feet away from me. "I've never hit you," he said flatly, his voice as dead as his stare. A small muscle twitched under his left eye.

"That doesn't matter," I replied. "You know your behavior is wrong. You intentionally try to scare me. Don't touch me again, don't get in my face, and don't scream at me. I am not responsible for your anger, and I'm done taking it."

There wasn't one moment that caused this shift inside me—it had been building over time. I had gradually grown stronger, and my relationship with Robert was shifting. I wasn't the woman who cowered when he was angry anymore.

Working for Mobile Crisis meant regular coordination with law enforcement, and I'd gotten to know a few local cops. One, Jamison, had become a friend. I could tell that made Robert uneasy.

"So, what are you going to do?" he asked, his voice thick with anger. "Call Jamison?"

"I will if you give me a reason," I said without hesitation.

His eye twitched again. He turned, storming off to the basement to blast his favorite Hendrix album.

My understanding of Robert—and people like him—had been growing over time, and in 2000, I finally had objective proof. The sewage treatment plant job had hit a dead end, and Robert complained about it constantly. I was still carrying most of the financial load and encouraged him to look for something else. That's when he applied for a job as a probation officer. His degree qualified him, and it came with good pay and benefits, though I was aware that he likely was not tempera-men-tally suited for it. I didn't think they'd hire him.

Though he did well in the interviews he needed to pass one final hurdle: a psychological evaluation, which included several personality tests. It was comprehensive and meant to be objective. The entire evaluation took several hours.

Robert was optimistic after the initial visit with the psychologist. He gave me a play-by-play of the meeting, which he reported had included jokes and laughter. I was relieved at the prospect of a more stable income but quietly remained skeptical.

Two weeks later, he came home waving a manila envelope in the air. His face was flushed with anger.

"Goddamn slimy motherfucker!" he shouted. "I'll sue the bastard!"

I took a deep breath, bracing myself. "What's that?"

"It's a copy of what he wrote about me. I didn't get the job. It's all a bunch of bullshit!"

He was furious. He thought the psychologist had liked him, that they'd bonded during the interview. But this wasn't like the private therapists who had only scratched the surface over the years. This psychologist had gone deeper, administering tests like the Minnesota Multiphasic Personality Inventory (MMPI), which is difficult to fool. The MMPI has a built-in lie scale that's designed to detect attempts at deception.

After Robert went to bed, I pulled out the report. I read through the 12-page document, feeling the weight of each sentence:

"This individual displays prominent Cluster B traits

classified in the Diagnostic and Statistical Manual of Mental Disorders. Cluster B personality disorders are characterized by dramatic, overly emotional, or unpredictable thinking or behavior. They are often described as the 'dramatic, emotional, and erratic' cluster."

It went on to outline four specific personality disorders:

1. Antisocial Personality Disorder (**ASPD**): Deceitful, manipulative, and reckless behavior, often with no remorse for breaking social norms.
2. Borderline Personality Disorder (**BPD**): Instability in relationships, self-image, and emotions, along with impulsivity and intense episodes of anger, depression, or anxiety.
3. Histrionic Personality Disorder (**HPD**): Excessive emotionality and attention-seeking, often uncomfortable when not the center of attention, and superficial emotions.
4. Narcissistic Personality Disorder (**NPD**): A grandiose sense of self-importance, a need for excessive admiration, and a lack of empathy. Exploits others to achieve personal goals.

Each of these descriptions could have been written specifically for Robert. He wasn't just one of them—he was *all* of them.

I'd read about these disorders for years in the DSM, but I had never thought to apply them to Robert. I'd searched for every other explanation for his behavior and had been blind to what was right in front of me. The veil had lifted. The evidence was in my hand.

That night, something broke inside me. The bond that had tied me to Robert for so long was finally severed. I realized that I was powerless to help him change. This wasn't ADHD, it wasn't bipolar disorder—this was about his character. And character doesn't change.

I started to visualize my life without him.

War Games

2000–2004

Robert continued working at the sewer plant, though constant conflicts with his supervisor made it uncertain how long he would stay. Despite his dissatisfaction, he wasn't looking for anything better. Meanwhile, I settled into an uneasy acceptance of what our life had become, letting go of any remaining delusions that things might change. But I saw the status quo as temporary.

With my kids grown and on their own, my fantasy shifted. I no longer dreamed of an ideal marriage but of living peacefully alone in a small house by the sea, surrounded by my four cats. My energy now went into my work, my friends, books, and dancing.

A mosaic of minor disconnections grew between us. I became increasingly detached from Robert, no longer seeking his attention or affection. I was happiest when he wasn't home, and I stopped feeding our relationship with suggestions or attempts to repair it. Any lingering threads that once tied us together unraveled—at least, on my end.

When he told me he loved me, I responded with a flat "Thank you." I didn't believe him, and I couldn't bring myself to say the words back. His actions felt like part of a larger con, one I no longer cared to figure out. I told him I wasn't committed to the marriage anymore, that too much damage had been done. But despite my emotional distance, Robert's rage hadn't disappeared. Now that I wasn't a safe target, he began venting it elsewhere.

At 46, Robert discovered online multiplayer first-person shooter games. He became obsessed, playing for hours on end. After work, he'd sit in my home office, glued to the monitor from 5:30 in the evening until well past midnight. Weekends were worse—he'd sit there all day, compulsively gaming, abandoning any interest in music, his guitar, or drums. But the games didn't soothe him. If anything, they fueled his volatility.

I watched as a man in his mid-forties screamed at his computer, cursing and pounding the desk when things didn't go his way. He played with faceless teenage boys from around the world, but when they killed his charac-ter—*the entire point of the game*—he'd take it personally. He'd retaliate with taunts and threats, his messages filled with venom: "FUCK YOU! YOU LITTLE PIECE OF SHIT! I'M GOING TO MURDER YOU!" he'd type in all caps, as if the virtual kill had been a personal attack.

It was ugly to watch, and I kept my distance.

One October morning, after picking up the shattered pieces of his keyboard from the night before, I had reached my breaking point. I wouldn't live like this anymore.

"I'm done, Robert," I said, my voice calm but resolute. "I want to move on. I'll help you find a place to rent, and we can split what's in the bank. I'm not asking for anything back, but I need peace. I want you to go."

For the first time in what felt like forever, relief washed over me as I finally spoke the words I had been holding inside for so long. I didn't wish him ill—I just didn't want to be his wife anymore.

Robert stared at me, his face a cold, silent mask, the same expression I'd seen countless times before. But this time, he didn't yell. He didn't get in my face or throw insults. Instead, he moved methodically, making toast and coffee as if nothing had changed. We left separately for work, but the weight of the moment lingered.

I braced myself for what might come later—for him to explode in anger when I got home, for the house to be filled with the blare of Hendrix, for something to be broken and scattered on the floor. I imagined he might break down, pathetic and pleading, begging me to change my mind.

But this time, I knew I wouldn't. And I think he knew that too.

PART V

"Psychopaths have an uncanny ability to spot and use 'nurturant' women—that is, those who have a powerful need to help or mother others. Many such women are in the helping professions—nursing, social work, counseling—and tend to look for the goodness in others while minimizing their faults."

Robert Hare
WITHOUT CONSCIENCE

Robert—Back to the Beginning

October 2004

I will never own that I'm a victim. I hate that word applied to me. It sounds fragile, and I'm not. But if I'm honest, I must admit that for 17 years, I lived with a man who terrified me with his fits of rage and violence. On an October morning, I told him I was getting a divorce; that night, he killed himself in a theatrical-staged hanging in the dining room.

I came home at 8 pm and walked straight into a horror movie. When I pulled up, I noticed the house was dark, which confused me because his car was in the driveway. I parked in the garage and entered the house through the side door rather than the front entrance, which I generally used. If I'd gone in the front, I would have seen the poster board taped to the front door with *"I'M IN THE DINING ROOM WAITING FOR YOU"* scrawled in red magic marker.

When I opened the door and called "hello," there was silence. Dread tightened my stomach as I entered the foyer, where I usually found lights and music. All was silent that night. Something was off. I'd find out once I walked through the dark to the dining room.

It was late October, almost Halloween, and with the way a spotlight had been positioned, his hanging body could be seen through the living room picture window by anyone looking in our direction from the rear of the house.

And just as he had planned, I lost my mind—for a while.

He'd spent time preparing. A paper bag with a receipt from the hardware store was still on the front seat of his truck in the driveway. The detective later explained that he'd needed a rope and hardware for the elaborate noose he'd fashioned.

The night was warm, but I couldn't stop shaking. Police radios squawked, and men in uniforms bustled through my home. A grim police detective in a polo shirt had instructed me to stay in my bedroom under the watch of two officers in blue who stood alongside my bed while they dealt with the body and ruled out that I hadn't somehow killed him. The cops remained silent, awkwardly staring at the ground and shifting their weight back and forth as the hours ticked by.

Men from the coroner's office arrived and left. They let me call a nearby friend, who came over to sit beside me on my bed. "I'm so sorry," I told Nancy as she cried with me. "I feel guilty about this awful mess. It's all my fault." She helped me make phone calls to my children, and I tearfully apologized to each of them.

The detective questioned me at various times. When had I last talked to him? *In the morning before work.* Had he made any threats? *None. He had been calm. He'd recently stopped therapy. We had relationship problems. I'd discussed divorce before I left for my office.*

The detective was taking notes on a small spiral notepad.

Friends from around the state and my three adult children arrived the next day. Everyone tried to comfort me and help me find my footing, but nothing worked—surreal hours blended into surreal days, nights, and weeks.

I couldn't track conversations, and my words failed to link into coherent sentences when I tried to speak. My consciousness seemed altered in ways I'd never experienced before. Everything was strange and unfamiliar as if I'd lost myself. I was perceiving the world through some horrifying distorted funhouse mirror. How could Robert be dead, and how could he have done this awful thing? The poster on the front door was the kicker. When the detective held it up to show me, I gasped, "He wrote that for me? This feels...mean."

"Yes, he nodded. "It was. It was mean."

I experienced sensory overload if I tried to leave the house. My heartbeat would race intermittently, and I had frequent episodes of shortness of breath. I was lost in a vortex of misery unlike anything I'd ever experienced. I was sure people could tell something was wrong just by looking at me.

☙ ☙ ☙

My first tendency now, all these years later, is still to blame myself—not for Robert's death but for being in the relationship. I asked myself why I married him after noticing so many red flags. Robert broke things when he was frustrated. He thrust fists through walls, his head through the door, smashed appliances and televisions, even his guitar. He screamed, threatened, and destroyed —and consistently blamed me for his anger. On one occasion, he kicked the family dog in the head, which is unforgivable. That still makes me sick. Any of those events should have been enough reason for me to exit. Some could have gotten him arrested.

My inner dialogue can be intensely self-critical, something Robert noticed and played upon effectively over the years. That's the way the cycle of violence works. I stayed because, on some level, he convinced me that his rageful behavior was my fault. *If only I hadn't complained about the volume of the music, he wouldn't have blown up and smashed the stereo.* It seems absurd now, but it was how my mind worked back then. *If I'm careful, he won't get angry. When he's better, this will all be different.*

In the early years, I believed he would change. I fully expected that the rageful, impulsive, and volatile part of him would be cured, leaving behind the warm, funny, and affectionate man I was attached to. I failed to understand that my naïve hopes about personality change were impossible.

What I know now that I didn't realize then is that

some of my strongest personality qualities served as a flashing neon sign indicating an easy mark to such a man: my compassion and empathy, loyalty, my tendency to think the best of people, a naïve belief that people could transform, and my vulnerability to shame and self-blame—all are risk factors for exploitation in a pathological relationship. Since I was raised with magical thinking, I was prone to sliding into unrealistic hope, and psychology eventually became my particular form of magic.

I came into the relationship with zero skills in setting boundaries to protect myself. I wasn't even aware I needed to. And that is on me.

Robert was 30 when I met him and couldn't maintain gainful employment even though he had a college degree in psychology and was healthy, intelligent, and charming. He'd been fired from every job he'd ever had, usually for anger-related problems and conflicts with authority. He was in debt and close to homelessness.

But I saw so much potential. Robert was outgoing, brilliant, and witty, a talented musician and writer—and he was invested in going to therapy. Most of all, he nurtured me during the good times, which were many. His older brother was a successful brain surgeon, and his sister was an accomplished attorney. I was convinced Robert would eventually find his path.

Robert claimed to have grown up in an abusive family, so his problems with anger made sense to me based on what I understood about the human mind at the time. I do not know how much of what he reported was true. His father, a physician, had killed himself at age 47, the same thing Robert did at the same age. We now understand that much about personality is carried in our DNA and that not all violent human behavior is the result of childhood trauma. It's more complicated than that. Multiple factors contribute, but there's no single thing that's causative.

I believed in the transformative power of psychotherapy and the unlimited potential for personal growth. Now, I realize I had embraced psychotherapy with a misguided fervor akin to religion. I looked at Robert through the flawed lens of potential. I fell in love with the man I thought he would *become*.

And then there was the flattery and the attention he heaped on me. No one had ever adored me the way he did. What I called "love" at the time filled a gaping need in my core. I'd been a child starved for attention and wrapped in shame. He told me I was intelligent and beautiful, and I soaked it up. Things felt wonderful— except when he was angry, which was often. Then, it was my role to calm him down and soothe him. After he became calm, he'd once again become a prince and shower me with affection.

Robert depended on me to regulate his moods, resulting in an intense but pathological bond. From moment to moment, I never knew which Robert I would find, and I became exceedingly careful.

Even though I was a newly divorced young mother with three children, working full time and attending grad school at night, I allowed him to move in without any clear commitment to his financial contribution to the household. I erroneously assumed he would be motivated to share expenses equally and be as motivated to achieve as I was. Even after his behavior proved this to be untrue, I married him with the naive belief that, eventually, therapy would correct his lack of motivation. Of course, it did not.

Robert's goal was to stay attached to me, and he did whatever it took. He charmed most therapists he saw the same way he'd charmed me. Over the years, I'd figured that out. I'd also figured out that psychotherapy is not magic, and none of my goals for Robert had ever been his goals for himself.

🌿 🌿 🌿

After I returned home from Palm Desert, I started therapy with a man named Patrick, a soft-spoken bespectacled man in his seventies who specialized in suicide and its aftermath. He became something of a father figure in my mind. As I sat on his brown leather couch, taking notes on a yellow legal pad, Patrick gazed over the top of his reading glasses and explained, "Self-blame is the quintessential adaptive response to the shock of trauma. It doesn't matter what it is—the trauma survivor always blames themself."

I wrote that down in the journal I carried with me.

"You were particularly prone to guilt because of your upbringing, and of course, Robert knew this about you —he knew you better than anyone. His suicide was a way to keep you from leaving him; he was willing to die to make it happen. He wanted to occupy your heart for the rest of your life. Remember—he specifically left that large poster on the door for you."

Patrick held the gaze, and I felt the truth in my

bones.

"Robert struggled in life long before he came to know you. You can have compassion for his struggle, but please realize you did not cause it. You were always powerless to cure it."

Patrick paused to let that sink in, then continued. "It isn't easy to extricate yourself from a relationship with a man like this. Leaving is dangerous. Sometimes, it's deadly. Shavaun, if he'd had access to a gun that night, it's likely he'd have killed you both."

PART VI

"Sometimes we are just the collateral damage in someone else's war against themselves."

Lauren Eden
THE LIONESS AWAKENS

Look What You Made Me Do

(TRUE STORIES)

I

When my cousin hanged himself in the bedroom
He wrote on his bare chest in magic marker
"Look in my eyes, Mother"
Because he knew she'd find his dead body when she
  came to call him for dinner.
He felt strangely omnipotent
When he fantasized about how the image he would
  leave burned onto her retinas
Would haunt her for the rest of her days.
If he'd had a gun, he would have shot himself in front
  of her
But he had to make do with a rope
And a black magic marker.

II

My neighbor shot himself in the head during a fight
  with his wife.
I'd heard her crying most nights when he screamed
  profanities at her.
I watched him die in their living room
And tried to help her wash the blood off her hands
As I wondered what to do about the chunks of gray
  brain on the floorboards.

III

My best friend's brother was arguing with his wife
And shot off his face with a shotgun.
He hadn't angled correctly and missed the brain,
And now lives a fairly content, if restricted, life (dinner parties are out of the question) addicted to prescription opioids.
She had to pick up the pieces of his face off the ground.
I'm told the mustache was still miraculously attached to the upper lip.

Fine Transparent Vapors

What peculiar work this is, professional listening.
Traveling roads where no one wants to go,
surgically dancing with tendrils of pain.

Wounded healers ourselves, we bear witness.
Is it hubris to think we make a difference?
Assuming that caring and attunement will help,

We show up, sensing contours, giving our best,
finding unexpected grace and small victories
in pale, stained radiance.

My story changes you; your story changes me,
mysteries unlocked, and histories rewritten.
Minds expand into a greater space,
we dance.

Perhaps listening is another form of prayer.
Perhaps it's the bond that becomes something sacred.
Stories connect hearts and then rise in the air
like fine transparent vapors.

How May I Help You?

(phone call to my office in 2013)

"**H**ello, this is the County Mental Health Crisis Line. I'm Shavaun Scott. How may I help you?"

"Yeah, I have a question about medication. How many Ambien does it take to kill you?"

"Woah, it sounds like you're struggling. Let's talk about this. What's your name?"

"I'm not telling you that, and I know you don't have caller ID on those County phones. I'm calling so you can listen to me die."

"Is anyone with you now? Where are you?"

"Oh, I'm home. Alone. And I'm taking two bottles of Ambien while I drink this bottle of wine. Here—you can hear me swallow some more".

"I can't pretend to know what you're experiencing or all you've been through, but I'm glad you called for help. I'm *sure it's hard to feel hopeful right now, maybe impossible, but I'd like to hold hope for you. I've felt hopeless many times in my life, and things have improved over time. I may be wrong, but I hope things will improve for you."*

"Nope, I don't believe that. You people have never helped me before, so fuck you all. I'm mad at the world. Here—I'm swallowing some more. That makes 60 pills. It shouldn't be long now. How do you like this conversation?"

"Hey, I'd love to sit down and have coffee with you and talk face-to-face for a while. I want to hear more and get to know you. I can come wherever you are. You could tell me how the system has let you down and how we can improve. You sound very depressed. I know the system is flawed, but I want us to do better."

"Oh sure, like you care. The doctor took away my Xanax for no good reason. You'd bring the cops and have me locked up. What would you have me do? Write in a journal? Go to a support group? I've done all that. You're only there to collect a paycheck. Fuck you all. I've been fucked over by everyone in my life... fuck... you... all... I'm... done..."

"I'm looking out a window right now, and I can see the sky. Can you see the sky where you are? It's so beautiful outside today. Is there a way you can get outside? Do you have a neighbor you can talk to?"

'I'm... lying... on... the... bathroom... floor. Getting... sleepy. Fuck... you... bitch"

"Look, it's not too late. I don't want to hang up, but it's not too late for you to call 911. They could get there in time. You don't have to go today; there's always another day if you're sure you need to leave like this. Hello?

I'm listening. Can you hear me? I'm right here. I'm looking out the window and holding hope for you. I can see the sky. It's beautiful. The trees are tall and green. I picture you standing tall, like a redwood, rooted in the ground and reaching up to the sky toward the sun. I'm still here. I'm listening. Keep breathing. Can you hear me?

Hello? I'm still here. Hello? I'm listening.

EPILOGUE

We can have powerful bonds with people who are not good for us. We often call this kind of pathological attachment "love," even though it's destructive. In truth, it's a trauma bond.

A healthy, loving attachment means our partner treats us with respect, compassion, kindness, openness, and honesty. This kind of love allows us to expand, not shrink.

However, destructive attachments are ubiquitous. My friend Leah recently told me about her first husband and the father of their children:

> *"He was angry one day, and I talked about leaving. He got his rifle and calmly started cleaning it and then loading it; he said he couldn't live like this anymore and told me he was going to kill me and the kids and then*

himself. I was terrified. I begged I made promises–whatever it took to calm him down. I talked about God and how only God should take life. I told him I'd make everything better. I comforted him. Then he cried, said he was sorry, and I held him."

How many times have I heard a woman describe comforting a man who abused and terrorized her? More than I can count. It's the classic theme in the cycle of intimate partner abuse. Because, in truth, there's a duality to most abusive people. The Dr. Jekyll/Mr. Hyde archetype is real. Such violent individuals have multiple ego states, some charming, some pathetic, and some murderous. The charmer is seductive, the child is pathetic, and the monster may kill somebody. You may encounter all three characters behind one face on the same day.

Studies in primate biology have revealed that displacement aggression reduces predators'
stress hormones. Humans share this quality. Why do some people behave abusively? It temporarily makes them feel better—and they get away with it.

I've led therapy groups for suicide survivors, and it's not uncommon to hear women share stories of abusive men shooting themselves in the head in front of their wives during an argument. This behavior is not the self-annihilation of chronic depression, the confusion of psychosis, or the desperation of terminal illness; it's the voice of rage and dominance. It's the final "Live with this, bitch" message of hatred.

When there has been a history of inter-partner abuse in a relationship, suicide can be viewed on the continuum of violence. Sometimes, the violent partner, who is most often male, kills himself. Take it up a notch, and he kills her, then himself. In the most extreme cases, he kills children, the woman, then himself. Such events usually occur when the female partner tries to leave the relationship.

And in the aftermath of the dirty bomb suicide, those who survive are indeed broken, at least for a while. They are practiced at blaming themselves for his bad behavior, including the violent way these men chose to die. Violence is a grenade that leaves many victims behind.

Women have been socialized as caretakers, too often sacrificing their own needs and wellbeing to soothe an erratic partner. Taking on the responsibility of trying to create stability and peace for a man who could kill us on a bad day is to become a prisoner. The outcome can be lethal when an exit from the relationship is attempted. Someone may die. It may be her; it may be him; it may be the kids. Sometimes it's all of them. Many women stay in abusive relationships because they sense this.

In September 2020, a new woman joined our group. An angry man she was divorcing drove 50 miles in the middle of the night to shoot himself in the face with a shotgun on her front doorstep when she opened the door. This kind of suicide is a hairsbreadth away from homicide. I understand this now.

※ ※ ※

My friends saved me. A month after Robert's death, when I went to stay in their home, they helped me understand that this kind of suicide is about rage, power, and control. It was about vengeance. I never could heal Robert. No therapist had the power to change his personality. It doesn't work that way. There was an aspect of malevolence to him that was beyond my comprehension, and I needed to understand that and feel anger about it to learn to become protective of myself. Robert took his own life at age 47, the same age his father had been when he did the same thing. He killed himself, but he did not kill me. Every day, I wake up grateful for my life.

※ ※ ※

My aunt Annie died of cancer despite her metaphysical belief in faith healing. She had a slow and painful passing. Jane died in an assisted living facility with Alzheimer's. For the last few years of her life, all she did was cry, and her family had trouble seeing how God's plan for her life had worked out to her benefit. Ida died in an institution for the mentally ill in Kansas. We'll never know where all the babies are buried.

Over the decades, as I came to understand my mother's profoundly difficult life journey, my resent-ment toward her turned to compassion. Considering the hand she'd been dealt, she did her best, and my heart hurts for all those who do not experience safety in their early years and for children forced by circumstances to grow up too fast in what can be a very mean world.

My father remarried a gentle, kind woman fifteen years after my mother's death, and I loved my step-mother dearly. She believed in me and told me I could accomplish anything. My stepmother died of cirrhosis when I was 34, and my father died of pneumonia a year later. Pieces of my parents will always live inside me. I try to treasure the good bits.

I am never free of grief; there is always a shard of sorrow in my heart, but I have grown around it. My losses have shaped my form, which can feel jagged and irregular. I have intentionally forgotten to remember the dates of all the deaths. If I allowed myself to remember, I'd be perpetually overwhelmed.

My children are grown and have always been remarkable people; their lives are free of drama. My two sons supported themselves through college and became computer engineers. They've both married stellar women. My daughter has chosen a creative path; she is artistic, incredibly kind, and loves animals as I do. They've all made conscious decisions not to have children, decisions which I can fully understand.

I have been in private practice for nearly 35 years. I love helping people connect the dots that link their histories to the present and come to understand their choices. Though psychotherapy can't accomplish miracles, it's often helpful. Stories need words; otherwise, they will haunt our dreams and drive our behavior without our awareness.

With a nose for sniffing out psychosis as well as abuse, I'm still driven to understand mental illness. It hits the low-income and uneducated particularly hard, leaving its victims and their children vulnerable. I learned from my aunts' lives that Schizophrenia and obsessive-compulsive disorder often manifest as spiritualism and religion, and when untreated, these conditions can ruin lives for generations. Poverty, magical thinking, and mental illness create a tight, deadly braid.

My family of origin was steeped in magical thinking, with various combinations of fundamentalism and mysticism layered with secrets. This resulted in tragically impaired judgment and failed coping strategies that kept me from developing more mature and effective ways to navigate life. I lived with shame about my past for decades, but I've come to acknowledge it as it was. I hope my experiences serve as a bridge for others. I know that just the telling of a story has the potential to bring change.

Ghosts don't live in the ether but often inhabit our DNA. We're all haunted by the spirits of our ancestors, but we carry more than one story about them and ourselves. There are stories of trauma, loss, healing, and overcoming; stories of endings, transformations, and new beginnings. Acknowledging the truth unflinchingly, understanding the resulting impact, and not perceiving ourselves as stuck in a permanent victim narrative eventually leads us to a better future. We are all in the process of re-authoring our lives.

I've sometimes wondered if there's another version of me who lives in a parallel universe, a version that never wore a blindfold or carried the burden of others' emotions and expectations. I can go down the rabbit hole imagining her life and pondering the lessons I might still learn from her.

We are all continually shaped by events that could potentially shatter us. However, by embracing the entirety of our struggles, we can hope to assimilate them into an eventual sense of completeness. We can become whole.

❧ ❧ ❧

I changed in many ways after Robert's suicide. I understand now that I am breakable and have embraced my nervous system's need for a gentler life. I still have a sensitive heart, but I protect it now. I've also learned to take no shit. Trust has to be earned.

I've settled in the forest of the Pacific Northwest, that green place with vibrant blue skies and tall trees I dreamed of as a child. I drink tea in my garden, where I grow lavender and chamomile among roses so red they look black. I share my heart with a gentle man who never raises his voice, my beloved dog, and three cats. I have not attended a religious service in 40 years and have no fear of devils. No longer troubled by insomnia or nightmares, I'm at peace with all I cannot know or control; I believe that wisdom comes with accepting the human condition just as it is.

Occasionally, I sense a benign echo from the past and linger with a softer childhood memory, something having nothing to do with heaven or hell or prayer. Sometimes, I listen as the owls call from my trees at night, and I dance barefoot in the grass, smiling at the man in the moon and his wife.

Shavaun Scott

Shavaun Scott is a licensed psychotherapist, author, and speaker with over three decades of experience in the field of mental health. She specializes in trauma recovery, the treatment of anxiety and depression, and the exploration of the psychological aspects of violence and criminal behavior.

In addition to her work as a therapist, Shavaun is a passionate advocate for mental health education, frequently lecturing and writing on topics related to emotional wellness, trauma, and the societal impact of violent crime.

Shavaun's writing blends her deep knowledge of psychology with a compassionate, accessible style that resonates with a wide audience. Her publications include articles, essays, and books that explore complex mental health issues, offering insights into the ways individuals can overcome adversity.

Also by **Shavaun Scott**

Non-Fiction

THE FORGOTTEN SURVIVORS OF
GUN VIOLENCE: WOUNDED
Routledge, 2023

THE MINDS OF MASS KILLERS:
UNDERSTANDING AND INTERRUPTING
THE PATHWAY TO VIOLENCE
McFarland, 2021

GAME ADDICTION:
THE EXPERIENCE AND THE EFFECTS
McFarland 2009

www.ingramcontent.com/pod-product-compliance
Lightning Source LLC
La Vergne TN
LVHW091328040325
805029LV00004B/158